# DOWN HOME

# DOWN HOME

Treasured Recipes *from* Our House to Yours *from the* West Point Junior Auxiliary

# DOWN HOME

## Treasured Recipes *from* Our House to Yours

Published by West Point Junior Auxiliary

Copyright © 2004 by
West Point Junior Auxiliary
P.O. Box 45
West Point, Mississippi 39773

This cookbook is a collection of favorite recipes, which are not necessarily original recipes.

Library of Congress Control Number: 2004106154
ISBN: 0-9753363-0-4

Edited, Designed, and Manufactured by
Favorite Recipes® Press
An imprint of

**RP**™

P.O. Box 305142
Nashville, Tennessee 37230
800-358-0560

Art Director: Steve Newman
Book Design: Brad Whitfield and Susan Breining
Project Editor: Linda Jones

Manufactured in the United States of America
First Printing: 2004
6,000 copies

# JUNIOR AUXILIARY PRAYER

Send us, O God, as Thy messengers
to the hearts without a home,
to lives without love, to the crowds without a guide.
Send us to the children whom none have blessed,
to the famished whom none have visited,
to the fallen whom none have lifted,
to the bereaved whom none have comforted.

Kindle Thy flame on the altars of our hearts,
that others may be warmed thereby; cause Thy light to shine
in our souls, that others may see the way: keep our sympathies
and insight ready, our wills keen, our hands quick
to help others in their need.

Grant us clear vision, true judgment, with great daring
as we seek to right the wrong; and so endow us with cheerful
love that we may minister to the suffering and forlorn even as
Thou wouldst. May the blessing of God Almighty, the Father,
the Son and the Holy Spirit, rest upon us and upon all our work.
May He give us light to guide us, courage to support us,
and love to unite us now and forever more.

# JUNIOR AUXILIARY SLOGAN

*"Care Today—Character Tomorrow"*

# ABOUT THE ARTIST
*Cindy O'Barr Davis*

The beautiful cover of this cookbook was painted by one of Mississippi's rising artists. Davis also drew the line art displayed throughout the cookbook. Cindy O'Barr Davis is a graduate of Mississippi State University with a BFA in Fine Arts with an emphasis in Painting and a minor in Graphic Design.

Davis grew up in Okolona, Mississippi, and currently resides and owns her own business in West Point, Mississippi. Davis Framing & Gallery is a custom frame shop and fine art gallery located on Historic Murph Row in downtown West Point that features art by local and regional artists.

Cindy is an associate member of the West Point Junior Auxiliary chapter. During her active membership status in our organization, Cindy left her artistic touch on many of our service projects. She was a key player in the organization and publication of the *Down Home* cookbook. She played a vital role in designing the layout of the KidTown park. Futhermore, she implemented the "Stop the Violence" service project and served as co-chair of the committee that coordinated the renovation of the Sally Kate Winters Home.

She designed the mural on the walls of the nursery in the Sally Kate Winters Home. Davis served as decorating chairman for three years during the Charity Ball, which is the West Point Junior Auxiliary's primary finance project.

Cindy Davis is also responsible for the photography of the section divider pages and of the back cover. Cindy devoted many hours of her valuable time, and we would like to express our appreciation once again for all of her help!

*We would like to dedicate this book to Cindy for all of her hard work and profound commitment to the West Point community.*

# WEST POINT JUNIOR AUXILIARY

Since its inception in 1941, the West Point Junior Auxiliary, Inc., has been an organization of caring and extraordinary women who have given so much of themselves in their own quiet and unselfish ways, and thus have touched the lives of countless needy children in our community.

As a member of the National Association of Junior Auxiliaries with 106 chapters, the West Point chapter has a membership of 150. All proceeds from the sale of this book will support the diverse projects of the organization, which will in turn benefit the children of West Point and Clay County.

# TABLE OF CONTENTS

The Sally Kate Winters Park is located next to the downtown area and features fountains, an old-fashioned bandstand, beautiful arbors with century-old wisteria vines, a romantic gazebo for lovers, and beautiful landscaping. Named for the late Sally Kate Winters, it is the heart of the Prairie Arts Festival held every year on Labor Day weekend.

# BREAKFAST & BREADS

## TOYS FOR TOTS

As an ongoing project every year, we make stuffed animals available to the Clay County Medical Center for the children who have been injured or admitted because of illness and need to be comforted in stressful situations. Nothing seems to warm a child's heart like a stuffed animal when they are scared. And we are proud to continue this service for the children of our community.

# Breakfast Bread Pudding

1 (1-pound) loaf sliced firm white bread
¼ cup (½ stick) butter
3 cups sliced peeled tart apples
2 tablespoons flour
2 tablespoons sugar
½ cup raisins
1 teaspoon cinnamon
4 eggs, lightly beaten
4 cups low-fat (1 percent) milk
½ teaspoon salt
6 tablespoons sugar

Trim the crusts from the bread. Cut the bread into ½-inch cubes. Butter a 9×9-inch baking dish. Melt the butter in a medium skillet. Add the apples. Cook for 15 minutes or until tender, stirring occasionally. Mix the flour and 2 tablespoons sugar in a bowl. Stir into the apple mixture. Cook for 1 minute or until thickened, stirring constantly. Stir in the raisins and cinnamon. Spoon into the prepared pan. Layer the bread cubes over the apples.

Combine the eggs, milk, salt and 6 tablespoons sugar in a medium bowl and mix well. Pour over the bread cubes. Press the bread cubes down into the milk mixture to absorb the mixture, using a spoon. Bake at 300 degrees for 1¼ hours or until golden brown and a knife inserted in the center comes out clean. Serve warm with Canadian bacon. (Note: You may chill for 8 to 12 hours before baking and bake for 15 minutes longer.)

SERVES 6

## Overnight Coffee Cake

1 (18-count) package
   frozen rolls
½ cup (1 stick)
   butter, melted
1 (4-ounce) package vanilla
   cook-and-serve pudding mix
½ cup packed brown sugar
1 cup chopped pecans

Place the frozen rolls in a tube pan. Drizzle with some of the butter. Mix the pudding mix and brown sugar together. Sprinkle over the rolls. Pour the remaining butter over the top. Sprinkle with the pecans. Place in a cold oven. Let stand for 8 to 12 hours. Bake at 350 degrees for 45 minutes. Invert onto a serving plate. Serve warm.

SERVES 18

## Bacon Quiche

1 unbaked (9-inch) pie shell
1 cup (4 ounces) shredded
   Swiss cheese
8 slices bacon, cooked
   and crumbled
3 eggs, beaten
1 cup milk
⅛ teaspoon nutmeg
1 tablespoon chopped onion
Salt and pepper to taste

Prick the pie shell with a fork. Bake at 350 degrees for 10 minutes. Sprinkle the prebaked pie shell with the cheese and bacon. Combine the eggs, milk, nutmeg, onion, salt and pepper in a bowl and beat well. Pour over the cheese and bacon. Bake for 35 minutes or until set. (Note: Make Ham Quiche by using 3/4 cup cubed cooked ham and 1 cup shredded Cheddar cheese instead of the bacon and Swiss cheese.)

SERVES 6 TO 8

13

# Holiday Sausage Wreath

1 pound bulk pork sausage
1 (13-ounce) can refrigerator pizza dough
1/2 cup (2 ounces) shredded Cheddar cheese

*Brown* the sausage in a skillet, stirring until crumbly; drain. Spread the dough into a rectangle on a greased baking sheet. Spread the sausage and cheese to the edges. Roll up to enclose the filling. Shape into a ring, sealing the ends together. Bake at 350 degrees for 20 minutes.

SERVES 24

# Breakfast Casserole

1 pound bulk pork sausage
1 (8-count) can crescent rolls
1 1/2 cups (6 ounces) shredded Monterey Jack cheese
1 1/2 cups (6 ounces) shredded sharp Cheddar cheese
6 eggs, beaten
3/4 cup milk

*Brown* the sausage in a skillet, stirring until crumbly; drain. Unroll the crescent roll dough. Place in a 9×13-inch baking dish, stretching the dough to cover the bottom of the dish. Layer the sausage over the dough. Sprinkle with the Monterey Jack cheese and Cheddar cheese. Beat the eggs and milk in a bowl. Pour over the layers. Bake at 350 degrees for 40 minutes or until set.

SERVES 6 TO 8

# Yummy Breakfast Casserole

2 (8-count) cans crescent
  roll dough
16 ounces cream cheese,
  softened
1 cup sugar

1 teaspoon vanilla extract
1/2 cup (1 stick) butter,
  melted
1/4 cup sugar
1 teaspoon cinnamon

*U*nroll 1 can of the dough. Place in a baking dish, stretching the dough to cover the bottom of the dish. Beat the cream cheese, 1 cup sugar and vanilla in a mixing bowl until smooth. Spread over the dough. Unroll the remaining can of the dough. Place over the cream cheese mixture to cover. Pour the melted butter over the top. Sprinkle with a mixture of 1/4 cup sugar and the cinnamon. Bake at 350 degrees for 20 to 30 minutes or until golden brown.

SERVES 6 TO 8

# Buttermilk Pancakes

2 eggs
2 cups buttermilk
2 cups flour
2 tablespoons sugar
2 teaspoons baking powder
1 teaspoon baking soda

1 teaspoon salt
1/4 cup (1/2 stick) unsalted
  butter, melted
2 tablespoons vegetable oil
1/2 teaspoon vanilla extract

*B*eat the eggs in a mixing bowl until frothy. Add the buttermilk, flour, sugar, baking powder, baking soda, salt, butter, oil and vanilla and beat until smooth. Pour 1/4 cup at a time onto a hot lightly greased griddle. Cook until brown on both sides, turning once. Serve hot with your favorite syrup.

MAKES ABOUT 15

# Stuffed French Toast

| 12 slices bread, crusts trimmed | 2 apples, sliced |
| and cubed | 1/2 cup water |
| 16 ounces cream cheese, cubed | 1/2 cup sugar |
| 10 eggs | 1/4 cup (1/2 stick) butter |
| 2 cups milk | 2 teaspoons cinnamon |

SERVES 6 TO 8

*L*ayer 1/2 of the bread, the cream cheese and the remaining bread in a baking dish. Beat the eggs and milk in a mixing bowl. Pour over the layers. Chill, covered, for 8 to 12 hours. Bake at 350 degrees for 40 minutes. Combine the apples, water, sugar, butter and cinnamon in a skillet. Cook until the apples are tender and the sauce is caramelized. Pour over the hot baked layer. Serve with your hot favorite syrup.

# Banana Nut Bread

| 1 1/4 cups self-rising flour | 1 cup sugar |
| 1/3 cup vegetable oil | 1/3 cup chopped pecans |
| 1 cup mashed bananas | |

SERVES 12

*C*ombine the flour, oil, bananas, sugar and pecans in a bowl and mix well. Spoon into a greased and floured 5×7-inch loaf pan. Bake at 350 degrees for 1 hour. Invert onto a wire rack to cool.

# Lemon Blueberry Poppy Seed Bread

1 (18-ounce) package bakery-style
  blueberry muffin mix
2 tablespoons poppy seeds
1 egg
3/4 cup water
1 tablespoon lemon zest
1/2 cup confectioners' sugar
1 tablespoon lemon juice

Rinse the blueberries from the mix with cold water; drain. Mix the muffin mix and poppy seeds in a bowl. Add the egg and water. Stir for 50 strokes or until moistened. Fold in the blueberries and lemon zest. Spoon into a greased and floured 4x8-inch loaf pan. Sprinkle with the topping from the mix. Bake at 350 degrees for 1 hour or until a wooden pick inserted in the center comes out clean. Cool in the pan for 10 minutes. Loosen the loaf from the sides of the pan. Cover the top with foil to help keep the topping intact. Invert the loaf and turn right side up on a wire rack, discarding the foil. Cool completely.

Combine the confectioners' sugar and lemon juice in a small bowl and mix until smooth. Drizzle over the loaf.

SERVES 12

# Poppy Seed Bread

| | |
|---|---|
| 3 cups flour | 1½ cups milk |
| 1½ teaspoons salt | ¼ cup poppy seeds |
| 1½ teaspoons baking powder | 1½ teaspoons vanilla extract |
| 2¼ cups sugar | 1½ teaspoons almond extract |
| 3 eggs | 1½ teaspoons butter flavoring |
| 1 cup plus 2 tablespoons | Orange Glaze (below) |
| vegetable oil | |

Combine the flour, salt, baking powder, sugar, eggs, oil, milk, poppy seeds and flavorings in a mixing bowl and beat for 2 minutes. Pour into 2 greased and floured 4×8-inch loaf pans. Bake at 350 degrees for 1 hour. Drizzle Orange Glaze over the hot loaves.

MAKES 2 LOAVES

## Orange Glaze

¾ cup confectioners' sugar
¼ teaspoon butter flavoring
¼ teaspoon vanilla extract
¼ cup orange juice

Combine the confectioners' sugar, butter flavoring, vanilla and orange juice in a small mixing bowl and beat until smooth.

# Mississippi Spice Muffins

4 cups flour
2 teaspoons baking soda
1 teaspoon salt
1 tablespoon cinnamon
2 teaspoons allspice
2 teaspoons cloves
1 cup (2 sticks) margarine, softened
2 cups sugar
2 eggs
2 cups unsweetened applesauce
1 cup chopped nuts
Confectioners' sugar for sprinkling

Sift the flour, baking soda, salt, cinnamon, allspice and cloves together. Cream the margarine and sugar in a mixing bowl until light and fluffy. Add the eggs and applesauce and beat well. Add the flour mixture and beat well. Stir in the nuts. Spoon into greased muffin cups. Bake at 350 degrees for 8 to 10 minutes or until golden brown. Sprinkle with confectioners' sugar.

MAKES ABOUT 2 DOZEN

# Homemade Bread

6 to 7 cups flour
3 tablespoons sugar
2¼ teaspoons salt
3 envelopes dry yeast
2¼ cups water
3 tablespoons butter

Combine 2 cups flour, the sugar, salt and yeast in a large bowl and mix well. Heat the water and butter in a saucepan until a candy thermometer registers 120 to 130 degrees. Add to the flour mixture. Beat at medium speed for 3 minutes. Stir in 3 to 3½ cups flour. Knead in the remaining 1 to 1½ cups flour on a generously floured surface for 10 to 12 minutes or until the dough is smooth and elastic. Place in a greased bowl, turning to grease the surface. Cover the bowl. Place the bowl in a pan of warm water. Let rise for 15 minutes.

Punch the dough down. Divide the dough into halves. Shape each half into a ball. Place each ball on a greased baking sheet. Cut a ¼-inch-deep lattice design in the top of each. Cover with a towel. Let rise in a warm place for 15 minutes or until doubled in bulk.

Bake at 400 degrees for 23 to 24 minutes or until golden brown. Remove to wire racks to cool.

MAKES 2 ROUND LOAVES

## Herb Focaccia

1 (11-ounce) can refrigerator French bread dough
2 tablespoons olive oil
1 teaspoon kosher salt
1 teaspoon pepper
1 teaspoon oregano
1 teaspoon basil
1/2 teaspoon thyme

*U*nroll the dough on a baking sheet and flatten slightly. Press the handle of a wooden spoon into the dough at 1-inch intervals to make indentations. Drizzle with the olive oil. Sprinkle with the kosher salt, pepper, oregano, basil and thyme. Bake at 375 degrees for 10 minutes. Cut into rectangles and serve warm.

SERVES 8

## Cheese Biscuits

2 cups baking mix
2/3 cup milk
1 cup (4 ounces) shredded Cheddar cheese
2 tablespoons butter, melted
1/8 teaspoon garlic powder

*C*ombine the baking mix, milk and cheese in a bowl and mix well. Drop by spoonfuls onto an ungreased baking sheet. Bake at 450 degrees for 8 to 10 minutes or until golden brown. Mix the butter and garlic powder in a bowl. Brush over the warm biscuits.

MAKES 9

# Angel Biscuits

1 envelope dry yeast        ¼ cup sugar
2 tablespoons lukewarm water   1 teaspoon salt
   2 cups buttermilk         1 teaspoon baking soda
   4 cups unsifted flour       1 cup shortening

1 tablespoon baking powder

Dissolve the yeast in the lukewarm water in a bowl. Let stand for 5 minutes. Stir into the buttermilk in a small bowl. Sift the flour, baking powder, sugar, salt and baking soda into a bowl. Cut in the shortening until crumbly. Add the buttermilk mixture and mix thoroughly. Knead on a floured surface to form a smooth dough. (The dough can be covered with waxed paper at this point and stored in the refrigerator until ready to bake. Let the dough come to room temperature before baking.) Roll the dough into a circle. Cut with a biscuit cutter. Place on a baking sheet. Bake at 400 degrees for 15 minutes.

MAKES 2 DOZEN

# Sour Cream Biscuits

2 cups baking mix   ½ cup sour cream
   ½ cup Sprite   2 tablespoons butter, melted

Combine the baking mix, Sprite and sour cream in a bowl and mix well. Pat into a circle on a lightly floured surface. Cut with a biscuit cutter. Dip in the butter. Place on a baking sheet. Bake at 400 degrees for 12 to 15 minutes or until golden brown.

MAKES 12 TO 15

## Broccoli Corn Bread

1 (10-ounce) package frozen chopped broccoli, thawed
1 (8-ounce) package corn bread mix
4 eggs, lightly beaten
2 cups (8 ounces) shredded cheese
1 small onion, chopped
½ cup (1 stick) margarine, melted

Combine the broccoli, corn bread mix, eggs, cheese, onion and margarine in a bowl and mix well. Spoon into a nonstick 5×9-inch loaf pan. Bake at 400 degrees for 20 minutes or until brown. Do not overbake.

SERVES 12

## Mexican Corn Bread

½ cup vegetable oil
3 eggs, beaten
1 (15-ounce) can cream-style corn
1⅓ cups milk
1 tablespoon sugar
3 cups self-rising cornmeal
3 or 4 hot chiles, chopped
1 onion, chopped
2 cups (8 ounces) shredded Cheddar cheese

Heat the oil in a cast-iron skillet in a 375-degree oven. Beat the eggs, corn, milk and sugar in a bowl. Add the cornmeal and mix well. Stir in the chiles, onion and cheese. Pour the hot oil into the batter and mix well. Pour the batter into the hot skillet. Bake for 45 to 60 minutes or until golden brown.

SERVES 8

# Hushpuppies

Vegetable oil for deep-frying
1 cup self-rising flour
1 egg    1 tablespoon sugar
1 large bell pepper, chopped    1 teaspoon baking powder
2 large onions, chopped    1½ cups milk
3 cups self-rising cornmeal

*H*eat the oil in a deep fryer over medium heat. Mix the egg, bell pepper and onions in a bowl. Add the cornmeal, flour, sugar and baking powder and mix well. Add the milk gradually, stirring until of the desired consistency. Drop by teaspoonfuls into the hot oil. Deep-fry until golden brown. Remove to paper towels to drain.

SERVES 8 TO 10

# Mayonnaise Rolls

1 cup self-rising flour
2 tablespoons mayonnaise
½ cup milk

*C*ombine the flour, mayonnaise and milk in a bowl and mix well. Pour into muffin cups sprayed with nonstick cooking spray. Bake at 450 degrees for 20 minutes or until golden brown.

MAKES 6

# Parmesan Rounds

1 (6-count) package hoagie buns
1 cup mayonnaise

⅓ cup grated Parmesan cheese
5 or 6 green onions, chopped
¼ to ½ teaspoon garlic powder
½ teaspoon Worcestershire sauce

Cut the bread into ¼-inch rounds. Place on a baking sheet. Bake at 350 degrees until lightly toasted. Cool completely. (You may make 1 week ahead and store in a sealable plastic bag.)

Combine the mayonnaise, Parmesan cheese, green onions, garlic powder and Worcestershire sauce in a bowl and mix well. Spread on the toasted rounds. Place on a baking sheet. Broil until the mixture melts. (You may double the topping mixture if desired.)

SERVES 10 TO 12

The Sally Kate Winters Home seeks to bring some of the humanity, love, and respect that may have been missing into the lives of children in need. The home is an emergency shelter for children who may be experiencing a family crisis, abuse, or neglect or be in danger of exploitation. Serving up to twelve children between the ages of birth and seventeen at any one time, the Sally Kate Winters Home provides a wholesome, home-like environment for up to sixty days. Forty percent of the operating budget is derived through contributions, fund-raisers, and organizations.

# APPETIZERS

## STOP THE VIOLENCE

As part of the National Association of Junior Auxiliaries' mission, the West Point Junior Auxiliary (WPJA) hopes to make a difference in the children's lives at the Sally Kate Winters Home through projects that invest not only money, but time to help stop the violence in the children's lives. Each month, the WPJA signs up to organize an activity night with the children at the Sally Kate Winters Home. We might take the children out to dinner or to a water theme park, or we might enjoy an evening in the home with the children and plan arts and crafts activities, order pizza, and watch movies.

Upon inception of the "Stop the Violence" service project, the WPJA recognized a need for some of the rooms in the home to be redecorated. Since the Sally Kate Winters Home did not have funds in its budget to finance the redecoration project, the WPJA called upon area sister chapters to help finance and help in the redecoration. Our first phase of the redecoration process was the nursery. As our theme for the nursery, we chose to paint life-size cartoon characters on the walls. We, along with our life and associate members, had a baby shower to re-supply the nursery with needed items. Our second phase of the project entailed the chapter redecorating the children's rooms upstairs by painting and supplying bedding, drapes, and linens.

Through the Sally Kate Winters Home, it has been satisfying to play a role in these children's lives. Through all of our hard work and dedication, even if we made one child smile, the project was well worth it.

# Stuffed Mushrooms

*Chef Carter Fraley, Anthony's Restaurant*

2 tablespoons chopped garlic
5 tablespoons butter
1/2 cup finely chopped mushroom stems
1 cup chopped peeled cooked shrimp
1 cup flaked crab meat
5 tablespoons white wine
1 1/2 teaspoons salt
1/2 teaspoon white pepper
1/2 cup heavy cream
5 tablespoons grated Parmesan cheese
16 ounces cream cheese, softened
Bread crumbs
48 medium mushroom caps
Butter for cooking

Sauté the garlic in 5 tablespoons butter in a large saucepan. Add the mushroom stems. Sauté until soft. Stir in the shrimp and crab meat. Add the wine, salt and white pepper and mix well. Cook for 5 minutes, stirring frequently. Add the cream. Cook until the mixture begins to simmer. The mixture will be thin at this point. Stir in the Parmesan cheese. Add the cream cheese a small amount at a time, cooking until smooth after each addition, stirring constantly. Stir in enough bread crumbs to thicken the mixture and then cool. Stuff into the mushroom caps. Cook the stuffed mushrooms in butter in a skillet until the mushroom caps are soft and the stuffing is heated through.

SERVES 10 TO 12

28

# Creamy Chicken Roll-Ups

4 chicken thighs, cooked
3 ounces cream cheese,
  softened
1 (4-ounce) can chopped
  black olives, drained
1 onion, chopped
1 cup (4 ounces) shredded
  Cheddar cheese
1/2 cup sour cream
2 (8-count) cans crescent rolls
Melted butter for brushing
Parmesan cheese for sprinkling

Chop the chicken, discarding the skin and bones. Process the chicken, cream cheese, olives, onion, Cheddar cheese and sour cream in a food processor until well mixed and pasty. Unroll the dough and separate into triangles. Place 2 tablespoons of the chicken mixture on each triangle and roll up. Place on a baking sheet. Brush with melted butter. Sprinkle with Parmesan cheese. Bake at 350 degrees for 25 minutes or until golden brown.

MAKES 16

# Bacon Cheese Crispies

1/2 cup (1 stick) margarine,
  softened
2 cups (8 ounces) shredded
  sharp Cheddar cheese
1 teaspoon Worcestershire
  sauce
1/4 teaspoon salt
1/4 teaspoon dry mustard
1/4 teaspoon hot sauce
1 1/4 cups flour
10 slices bacon, cooked and
  finely crumbled

Combine the margarine, cheese, Worcestershire sauce, salt, dry mustard and hot sauce in a large bowl and mix well. Stir in the flour and bacon. Shape into 4 rolls about 6 inches long and 1 inch in diameter. Wrap in waxed paper. Chill for at least 8 hours. Unwrap the rolls and cut into slices 1/4 inch thick. Place on a lightly greased baking sheet. Bake at 375 degrees for 10 minutes or until light brown. Cool on a wire rack.

MAKES 6 DOZEN

29

# Ham and Cheese Puffs

2 cups baking mix    1/2 teaspoon salt
3/4 cup chopped cooked ham    2/3 cup milk
1 cup (4 ounces) shredded    1 egg
   Cheddar cheese    1/4 cup sour cream
1/2 cup finely chopped onion
   (optional)

Combine the baking mix, ham, cheese, onion, salt, milk, egg and sour cream in a bowl and mix well. Spread in a greased 9×13-inch baking dish or spoon into miniature muffin cups. Bake at 350 degrees for 25 to 30 minutes or until golden brown.

**SERVES 8**

# Mississippi Sin

1 1/2 cups sour cream    1/3 cup chopped green onions
8 ounces cream cheese,    1/2 cup chopped green chiles
   softened    1/2 cup chopped cooked ham
2 cups (8 ounces) shredded    Dash of Worcestershire sauce
   Cheddar cheese    1 loaf Hawaiian bread

Combine the sour cream and cream cheese in a bowl and mix well. Stir in the Cheddar cheese, green onions, green chiles, ham and Worcestershire sauce. Cut the top from the bread. Scoop out the inside to form a bread shell, reserving the bread. Cut the reserved bread into bite-size pieces. Pour the cheese mixture into the bread shell. Wrap in foil. Bake at 350 degrees for 1 hour. Serve with the bread pieces or crackers for dipping.

**SERVES 8**

# Sausage Balls

1 pound hot bulk pork sausage
1 pound sharp Cheddar cheese, shredded
3 cups baking mix

Combine the sausage, cheese and baking mix in a bowl and mix well. Shape into small balls. Place on a baking sheet. Bake at 400 degrees for 15 minutes or until golden brown.

MAKES ABOUT 75

# Beer Cheese

12 ounces sharp Cheddar cheese, shredded
8 ounces cream cheese, softened
1 garlic clove, minced
1 tablespoon Worcestershire sauce
1/2 teaspoon cayenne pepper
1/2 teaspoon dry mustard
1 cup beer

Process the Cheddar cheese and cream cheese in a food processor or blender until smooth. Add the garlic, Worcestershire sauce, cayenne pepper and dry mustard and process well. Add the beer gradually, processing constantly until blended. Spoon into a serving bowl. Chill, covered, for 1 hour. Serve with crusty bread, crackers or pretzel twists.

MAKES 2 1/2 CUPS

1 (8-ounce) package sharp Cheddar cheese cubes
1 (8-ounce) package Monterey Jack cheese cubes
1 medium jar green olives, drained
1 (3-ounce) can small pitted black olives, drained
1/2 bottle Italian salad dressing

Combine the Cheddar cheese cubes, Monterey Jack cheese cubes, green olives, black olives and salad dressing in a bowl and toss to mix. Chill, covered, for at least 2 hours before serving. Serve with assorted crackers.

SERVES 8

## Tuna Cheese Ball

8 ounces cream cheese, softened
1 cup (4 ounces) shredded Cheddar cheese
1/4 cup creamy cucumber dressing
1 (9-ounce) can tuna, drained
1 teaspoon dill weed
1/4 cup finely chopped parsley

Combine the cream cheese, Cheddar cheese, cucumber dressing, tuna and dill weed in a bowl and mix well. Chill in the refrigerator. Shape into a ball. Roll in the chopped parsley. Garnish with additional parsley. Serve with crackers.

SERVES 8

# Ground Beef Dip

1 pound ground beef
3 bunches green onions, chopped
1 (14-ounce) can stewed tomatoes
1 (10-ounce) can tomatoes with green chiles
1 (6-ounce) can tomato paste
¾ cup diced pimentos
1 teaspoon chili powder
Oregano to taste
Pepper to taste
Garlic to taste
¾ cup slivered almonds
8 ounces Cheddar cheese, shredded

*B*rown the ground beef and green onions in a skillet, stirring until the ground beef is crumbly. Add the stewed tomatoes, tomatoes with green chiles, tomato paste, pimentos, chili powder, oregano, pepper and garlic and mix well. Stir in the almonds and cheese. Spoon into a baking dish. Bake at 350 degrees for 45 minutes. Serve with corn chips for dipping.

SERVES 8

33

# Guacamole Dip

2 ripe avocados, peeled and chopped
1 onion, finely chopped
1 or 2 green chiles, finely chopped
1 tablespoon lemon juice
1 teaspoon salt
1/2 teaspoon coarsely ground pepper
1/2 teaspoon Fruit-Fresh
1 tomato, finely chopped

*Beat* the avocados, onion, green chiles, lemon juice, salt, pepper and Fruit-Fresh in a bowl until creamy. Stir in the tomato. Chill, covered, for at least 1 hour before serving. Serve with chips.

MAKES ABOUT 2 CUPS

## Pico de Gallo

4 large tomatoes, finely chopped
4 onions, finely chopped
1 bunch fresh cilantro, finely chopped
2 (16-ounce) cans Mexican stewed tomatoes, drained and chopped
1 (16-ounce) jar medium picante sauce
Salt and pepper to taste

*Combine* the tomatoes, onions, cilantro, stewed tomatoes, picante sauce, salt and pepper in a large bowl and mix well. Serve with chips for dipping.

MAKES 8 TO 10 CUPS

# Vidalia Onion Cheese Dip

3 large Vidalia onions, coarsely chopped
2 tablespoons unsalted butter
1 cup mayonnaise
8 ounces sharp Cheddar cheese, shredded
1/2 teaspoon Tabasco sauce
1 garlic clove, minced

Sauté the onions in the butter in a skillet until translucent. Stir in the mayonnaise, cheese, Tabasco sauce and garlic. Spoon into a buttered baking dish. Bake at 375 degrees for 25 minutes. Serve with potato chips, tortilla chips or crackers.

SERVES 12 TO 15

# Taco Dip

1 cup chopped cooked chicken
2 cups (8 ounces) shredded sharp Cheddar cheese
1 cup sour cream
1 (4-ounce) can chopped green chiles, drained
1 envelope taco seasoning mix
1/2 (10-ounce) can corn

Combine the chicken, cheese, sour cream, green chiles, taco seasoning mix and corn in a bowl and mix well. Chill, covered, for 1 hour. Serve with crackers or tortilla chips.

MAKES 4 CUPS

# Ranch Chicken Dip

8 ounces cream cheese, softened
1 envelope ranch salad dressing mix
1 (5-ounce) can chicken, drained

Combine the cream cheese, salad dressing mix and chicken in a mixing bowl and beat well. Serve with assorted crackers.

**SERVES 8**

# Seafood Appetizer

8 ounces cream cheese, softened
2 tablespoons mayonnaise
1 tablespoon Worcestershire sauce
Garlic powder to taste
1 (6-ounce) can crab meat, drained
1 (4-ounce) can shrimp, drained
1 (12-ounce) bottle chili sauce
4 or 5 drops of Tabasco sauce
Horseradish to taste

Combine the cream cheese, mayonnaise, Worcestershire sauce and garlic powder in a bowl and mix until smooth. Spread in a glass pie plate. Layer the crab meat and shrimp over the cream cheese layer. Mix the chili sauce, Tabasco sauce and horseradish in a bowl. Spread over the top. Serve with corn chips or assorted crackers.

**SERVES 8 TO 10**

# Layered Shrimp Dip

3 ounces cream cheese, softened
6 tablespoons salsa
½ cup cocktail sauce
1 (4-ounce) can small shrimp, drained
1 (2-ounce) can sliced black olives, drained
1 cup (4 ounces) shredded Cheddar cheese
1 cup (4 ounces) shredded Monterey Jack cheese
Sliced green onions

*B*lend the cream cheese and 3 tablespoons of the salsa in a bowl until smooth. Spread onto a serving plate. Mix the remaining salsa and the cocktail sauce in a bowl. Spread over the cream cheese layer. Continue layering with the shrimp and olives. Mix the Cheddar cheese and Monterey Jack cheese together and sprinkle over the olives. Sprinkle with green onions. Serve with tortilla chips.

SERVES 8 TO 10

# Shrimp Dip

8 ounces cream cheese, softened
1 cup sour cream
1/2 onion, finely chopped
Mayonnaise to taste
Juice of 1 lemon
Salt and pepper to taste
2 (4-ounce) cans shrimp, drained

*Beat* the cream cheese and sour cream in a mixing bowl until smooth. Fold in the mayonnaise. Stir in the onion and lemon juice. Season with salt and pepper. Mash the shrimp with a fork in a bowl. Add to the cream cheese mixture and mix well. Spoon into a serving bowl. Chill, covered, for several hours to allow the flavors to blend. Serve with corn chips or crackers, or use as a spread for sandwiches.

SERVES 8

# Monterey Jack Salsa

1 (4-ounce) can chopped green chiles, drained
1 (3-ounce) can chopped black olives, drained
4 green onions, chopped
4 ounces Monterey Jack cheese, shredded
1 tomato, chopped
1/2 cup Italian salad dressing
1/4 cup chopped fresh cilantro

*Combine* the green chiles, olives, green onions, cheese, tomato, salad dressing and cilantro in a bowl and mix well. Spoon into a serving bowl. Serve with tortilla chips.

SERVES 4 TO 6

# Caramel Dip

½ cup (1 stick) butter
1½ cups packed brown sugar
¾ cup light corn syrup
1 (14-ounce) can sweetened condensed milk
1 teaspoon vanilla extract
¼ teaspoon cinnamon
Pinch of salt

Combine the butter, brown sugar, corn syrup and condensed milk in a saucepan. Cook over medium heat for 5 minutes or until the brown sugar is dissolved, stirring constantly. Stir in the vanilla, cinnamon and salt. Pour into a serving bowl. Serve with sliced apples for dipping.

MAKES ABOUT 4 CUPS

# Honey Fruit Dip

1 (7-ounce) jar marshmallow creme
8 ounces cream cheese, softened
⅓ cup honey

Whip the marshmallow creme and cream cheese in a mixing bowl until smooth. Add the honey and mix well. Serve with sliced fresh fruit for dipping.

MAKES 2 CUPS

39

# Banana Slush Punch

6 cups water
4 cups sugar
1 (46-ounce) can pineapple
   juice
1 (6-ounce) can frozen
   lemonade concentrate
1 (12-ounce) can frozen
   orange juice concentrate,
   prepared
5 bananas, mashed
12 liters lemon-lime soda or
   ginger ale, chilled

*Heat* the water and sugar in a large saucepan until the sugar dissolves, stirring occasionally. Remove from the heat to cool. Combine the sugar water, pineapple juice, lemonade concentrate and orange juice in a large freezer-proof container and blend well. Stir in the bananas. Freeze until firm. Remove from the freezer and let stand at room temperature for 1 hour or until softened. To serve, scoop 1/3 of the mixture into a punch bowl. Pour 4 liters of the lemon-lime soda over the top. Return the remaining mixture to the freezer. Replenish the punch bowl as needed with the remaining frozen mixture and lemon-lime soda. (Note: You may add a splash of rum.)

SERVES 50

# Christmas Brunch Punch

1½ teaspoons whole cloves
1 cinnamon stick
3 cups pineapple juice
3 cups cranberry juice
1½ cups water
1/3 cup packed brown sugar
1/8 teaspoon salt

*Combine* the whole cloves and cinnamon stick in a percolator basket. Combine the pineapple juice, cranberry juice, water, brown sugar and salt in a percolator. Perk using the manufacturer's instructions. (To increase the amount of servings to 30, increase the pineapple juice and cranberry juice to 9 cups each, the water to 4¼ cups, the brown sugar to 1 cup, the cloves to 4½ teaspoons, the cinnamon to 4 sticks and the salt to ¼ teaspoon.)

SERVES 10

## Sherbet Punch

1 gallon lime or orange sherbet
4 liters lemon-lime soda or ginger ale, chilled
1 gallon red fruit punch, chilled

Cut the sherbet into cubes using a cheese wire and place in a punch bowl. Add the lemon-lime soda and fruit punch. Ladle into punch cups. (Note: To make a punch bowl ring, freeze 1 quart red fruit punch with maraschino cherries in a bundt pan. Invert into the punch bowl for decoration.)

SERVES 50

## Tea Punch

3 quarts water
8 tea bags
1 (12-ounce) container frozen lemonade, thawed
1 (32-ounce) bottle ginger ale, chilled

Bring the water to a boil in a large teapot. Add the tea bags. Steep until the tea is the desired strength. Blend the tea and lemonade concentrate in a large container. Chill in the refrigerator. Stir in the ginger ale just before serving.

SERVES 15

41

*The Bryan Public Library, located in the heart of downtown West Point, serves as the headquarters of the Tombigbee Regional Library System, which encompasses libraries in four northeast Mississippi counties: Clay, Monroe, Choctaw, and Webster. Mary Helen Waggoner serves as the director.*

*Constantly innovating, the Library is connected to a high-speed telecommunications network that offers public Internet accessibility and an automated circulation system with over 116,000 titles. The Library also provides access to the Magnolia databases, which is a state-funded library consortium providing online databases for public schools, public libraries, community college libraries, and university libraries in Mississippi. Regional system connectivity and interlibrary loan programs with our two universities expand Bryan's available titles and services to levels that exceed those of many large cities.*

# VEGETABLES & SIDE DISHES

## READING IS FUNDAMENTAL, INC.

*Reading Is Fundamental, Inc. (RIF), prepares and motivates children to read by delivering free books and literacy resources to children and families. Founded in 1966, RIF is the oldest and largest children and family nonprofit organization in the United States. The West Point Junior Auxiliary has partnered with the National Reading Is Fun Organization to distribute these books to the children of West Point. WPJA distributes books to students from pre-kindergarten through sixth grade. Additionally, as the books are distributed, the WPJA encourages children to read...that reading is the fundamental key to success in life. The children enjoy the excitement of choosing a book to keep as their own. WPJA is proud to serve all the children in Clay County.*

# Sesame Asparagus

6 asparagus spears, trimmed
1/4 teaspoon salt
1 teaspoon butter, melted
1 teaspoon lemon juice
3/4 teaspoon sesame seeds

*Place* the asparagus in a skillet. Season with the salt. Add enough water to cover. Bring to a boil and reduce the heat. Simmer, covered, for 4 minutes or until tender-crisp; drain. Combine the butter, lemon juice and sesame seeds in a small bowl and mix well. Drain the asparagus and place in a serving dish. Drizzle with the butter mixture. (Note: Increase the salt, butter, lemon juice and sesame seeds for every 6 spears of asparagus used.)

SERVES 2

# Butter Beans with Bacon and Tomatoes

3 slices bacon
1 onion, finely chopped
1 small green bell pepper, chopped
3 garlic cloves, minced
1 bay leaf (optional)
3 tomatoes, chopped
4 cups chicken broth
4 cups fresh or frozen butter beans, thawed
2 tablespoons minced fresh parsley
1 teaspoon salt
1 teaspoon pepper
1 teaspoon Worcestershire sauce
1/2 teaspoon hot sauce

Cook the bacon in a Dutch oven until crisp. Stir in the onion, bell pepper, garlic and bay leaf. Sauté until the vegetables are tender. Stir in the tomatoes. Cook for 3 minutes. Stir in the chicken broth and butter beans. Bring to a boil. Cover and reduce the heat. Simmer for 30 minutes, stirring occasionally. Simmer, uncovered, for 20 minutes, stirring frequently. Stir in the parsley, salt, pepper, Worcestershire sauce and hot sauce. Cook for 5 minutes, stirring frequently. Discard the bay leaf before serving.

SERVES 4 TO 6

# Mom's Baked Beans

3 large cans pork and beans, drained
1 (1-pound) package dark brown sugar
3 tablespoons prepared mustard
2 large onions, chopped or thinly sliced
1 pound sliced bacon

Combine the pork and beans, brown sugar, mustard and onions in a large bowl and mix well. Spoon into a large baking dish. Cover the top with the bacon. Bake at 350 degrees for 1 1/2 hours or until the onions are tender and the bacon is crisp. (Note: You may use a case of regular-size cans of pork and beans if desired.)

SERVES 12 TO 16

# Baked Beans with Ground Beef

1 pound ground beef    1/4 cup light corn syrup
2 large cans pork and beans    3 tablespoons brown sugar
1 small onion, minced    Salt and pepper to taste
1/4 cup ketchup

Brown the ground beef in a skillet, stirring until crumbly; drain. Combine the ground beef, pork and beans, onion, ketchup, corn syrup, brown sugar, salt and pepper in a large bowl and mix well. Spoon into a large baking dish. Bake at 350 degrees for 45 minutes.

SERVES 6 TO 10

# Four-Bean Pot

8 ounces sliced bacon, chopped
2½ cups chopped onion
1 (16-ounce) can kidney beans, drained
1 (16-ounce) can butter beans, drained
1 (16-ounce) can lima beans, drained
2 (16-ounce) cans pork and beans
½ cup cider vinegar
1 teaspoon garlic powder
1 teaspoon dry mustard

Sauté the bacon and onion in a large skillet until the bacon is crisp; drain. Add the kidney beans, butter beans, lima beans, pork and beans, vinegar, garlic powder and dry mustard and mix well. Spoon into a large bean pot or baking dish. Bake at 350 degrees for 1 hour or until bubbly. Let stand for 20 minutes before serving.

SERVES 20

47

# Tangy Green Bean Bundles

12 ounces sliced bacon
2 (15-ounce) cans whole green beans
3 tablespoons butter
1 tablespoon white vinegar
2 tablespoons tarragon vinegar
1 teaspoon salt
1 teaspoon paprika
1 tablespoon parsley
1 teaspoon grated onion

SERVES 8

Cut the bacon slices into halves. Wrap 6 to 9 green beans with a bacon half and secure with a wooden pick. Repeat with the remaining beans and bacon. Place on a rack in a broiler pan. Broil until the bacon is crisp. Combine the butter, white vinegar, tarragon vinegar, salt, paprika, parsley and onion in a saucepan and mix well. Bring just to a boil. Place the green bean bundles in a serving dish. Pour the hot sauce over the top.

# Stir-Fried Green Beans

12 ounces fresh green beans, trimmed
2 tablespoons salt
1 tablespoon vegetable oil
1 onion, sliced and separated into rings
3 large garlic cloves, peeled
2 tablespoons water
1 teaspoon sugar
1/2 teaspoon basil
1 teaspoon salt
2 tablespoons freshly grated Parmesan cheese

Cut the green beans into halves if over 4 inches long. Bring 1 inch of water to a boil in a large heavy skillet over high heat. Add 2 tablespoons salt and the green beans. Cook, covered, for 5 minutes or until tender but still slightly firm. Do not overcook. Drain and rinse immediately with cool water to stop the cooking process.

Heat the oil in a large heavy skillet over high heat. Add the onion and garlic. Reduce the heat to medium-high. Sauté for 4 to 5 minutes or until the onion is brown. Add the green beans. Stir-fry for 1 minute. Stir in 2 tablespoons water, the sugar, basil and 1 teaspoon salt. Stir-fry for 1 to 2 minutes longer. Discard the garlic. Sprinkle the green beans with the Parmesan cheese. Serve hot.

SERVES 4

49

# Broccoli Casserole

2 (10-ounce) packages frozen chopped broccoli
1 (10-ounce) can cream of mushroom soup
1 cup mayonnaise
1 onion, chopped
2 eggs, beaten
Salt and pepper to taste
1 cup (4 ounces) shredded mild or sharp Cheddar cheese
1/4 cup (1/2 stick) margarine, melted
1/2 package herb stuffing

Cook the broccoli using the package directions; drain. Add the soup, mayonnaise, onion, eggs, salt and pepper. Spoon into a 1 1/2-quart baking dish. Sprinkle with the cheese. Drizzle with the melted margarine. Cover the top with the stuffing. Bake, uncovered, at 350 degrees for 45 minutes.

SERVES 8

# Broccoli and Rice Casserole

1 (10-ounce) package frozen chopped broccoli,
    cooked and drained
1 cup rice, uncooked
1 jar jalapeño cheese spread
1 (10-ounce) can cream of mushroom soup
1 (10-ounce) can cream of chicken soup
Shredded Cheddar cheese for topping

Combine the broccoli, rice, cheese spread, mushroom soup and chicken soup in a bowl and mix well. Spoon into a baking dish. Bake at 350 degrees for 30 minutes. Remove from the oven and sprinkle with Cheddar cheese.

SERVES 6 TO 8

## Cajun Carrots

10 to 12 whole carrots, peeled and sliced
Salt to taste
8 green onions, chopped
6 tablespoons butter
1½ tablespoons brown sugar
Cream to taste

*B*oil the carrots in enough salted water to cover in a saucepan until tender; drain. Sauté the green onions in the butter in a skillet until tender. Add the sautéed green onions and brown sugar to the carrots and mash until smooth. Add enough cream to make of the desired consistency, beating constantly.

SERVES 6 TO 8

## Corn Casserole

1 (8-ounce) package yellow rice
1 (11-ounce) can Mexicorn
1 (10-ounce) can cream of mushroom soup
1 cup sour cream
Shredded cheese for sprinkling

*C*ook the rice using the package directions. Add the Mexicorn, soup and sour cream and mix well. Spoon into a baking dish. Sprinkle with cheese. Bake at 400 degrees for 20 minutes.

SERVES 6 TO 8

51

# Shoe Peg Corn Casserole

1/2 cup (2 ounces) shredded
   Cheddar cheese
1 (11-ounce) can
   Shoe Peg corn
1 (16-ounce) can French-style
   green beans, drained
1/2 cup chopped onion
1/2 cup chopped celery

1 cup sour cream
1 (10-ounce) can cream of
   celery soup
1/2 cup (1 stick) butter,
   melted
1 sleeve butter crackers,
   crumbled
1/2 green bell pepper, chopped

Combine the cheese, corn, green beans, onion, celery, sour cream and soup in a bowl and mix well. Spoon into a 9×12-inch baking dish. Pour the melted butter over the mixture. Spread the cracker crumbs over the top. Bake at 350 degrees for 30 to 40 minutes or until bubbly.

SERVES 6 TO 8

# Eggplant Casserole

1 onion, chopped
2 garlic cloves, minced
3 tablespoons butter
3 tablespoons vegetable oil
2 cups chopped tomatoes
1/4 teaspoon salt
1/4 teaspoon pepper

1/4 teaspoon thyme
1/4 cup chopped parsley
1/4 cup soft bread crumbs
2 medium eggplant, peeled
   and coarsely chopped
1/2 cup (2 ounces) shredded
   mozzarella cheese

Sauté the onion and garlic in the butter and oil in a skillet. Add the tomatoes, salt, pepper, thyme and parsley. Bring to a boil. Stir in the bread crumbs. Place the eggplant in a greased baking dish. Broil until tender, stirring frequently. Add the tomato mixture. Sprinkle with the cheese. Bake at 350 degrees for 30 minutes.

SERVES 6 TO 8

## Baked Onion Slices

1 onion, cut into 1/4-inch slices
1 onion, chopped
1 cup heavy cream
1 tablespoon flour
1 sleeve butter crackers, crumbled
Parmesan cheese to taste
6 tablespoons butter

*L*ayer the sliced onion and chopped onion in a baking dish sprayed with nonstick cooking spray. Mix the cream and flour in a bowl. Pour over the onions. Sprinkle the top with the butter cracker crumbs and Parmesan cheese. Dot with the butter. Bake at 350 degrees for 45 minutes. Serve carefully with a large spatula.

SERVES 4

## Blue Cheese Potatoes

2 pounds red potatoes, cut into chunks
1/4 cup whipping cream, whipped
1/4 cup crumbled blue cheese
1 cup mayonnaise
8 ounces sliced bacon, cooked and crumbled

*P*lace the potatoes in a large saucepan and cover with water. Bring to a boil over medium-high heat. Cook, covered, for 15 to 20 minutes or until tender; drain. Fold the whipped cream and blue cheese into the mayonnaise in a bowl. Stir the blue cheese mixture gently into the hot potatoes. Spoon into a serving dish. Sprinkle with the bacon.

SERVES 6 TO 8

# Hash Brown Casserole

1 bunch green onions, chopped
3 garlic cloves, minced
1 (10-ounce) can cream of celery soup
1 cup sour cream
½ cup (1 stick) butter, softened
2 cups (8 ounces) shredded Cheddar cheese
1 (32-ounce) package southern-style hash browns
1 pound sliced bacon, cooked and crumbled

Sauté the green onions and garlic in a nonstick skillet. Combine the soup, sour cream, butter and cheese in a bowl and mix well. Stir in the green onion mixture. Place the hash browns in a 9×13-inch baking dish. Spoon the cheese mixture over the top. Sprinkle with the bacon. Cover with foil. Bake at 350 degrees for 1¼ hours.

SERVES 8 TO 10

# Party Potatoes

3 or 4 large baking potatoes, baked and cooled
1 cup sour cream
⅓ cup chopped green onions
2 tablespoons butter
1 cup (4 ounces) shredded medium-sharp Cheddar cheese
1½ teaspoons salt
Pepper to taste

Peel the baked potatoes. Grate the potatoes into a large bowl. Add the sour cream, green onions, butter and cheese and mix well. Season with the salt and pepper. Spoon into a baking dish. Chill, covered, for 8 to 12 hours. Bake at 350 degrees for 30 minutes. (Note: This recipe freezes well.)

SERVES 6 TO 8

# Spinach and Artichokes in
## Puff Pastry

1 (17-ounce) package frozen puff pastry
1 (10-ounce) package frozen chopped spinach, thawed
1 (14-ounce) can marinated or plain artichoke hearts,
  drained and chopped
½ cup mayonnaise
½ cup (2 ounces) grated Parmesan cheese
1 teaspoon onion powder
1 teaspoon garlic powder
½ teaspoon pepper

Thaw the puff pastry at room temperature for 30 minutes. Drain the spinach well, squeezing out all of the liquid by pressing between paper towels or squeezing by hand. Combine the spinach, artichoke hearts, mayonnaise, cheese, onion powder, garlic powder and pepper in a bowl and mix well. Unfold 1 pastry sheet and place on a lightly floured surface or on heavy-duty plastic wrap. Spread ½ of the spinach mixture evenly over the pastry, leaving a ½-inch border. Roll up to enclose the filling, pressing the seam to seal. Wrap in heavy-duty plastic wrap. Repeat the procedure with the remaining pastry sheets and spinach mixture. Freeze for 30 minutes. Cut into slices ½ inch thick. Place on a baking sheet. Bake at 400 degrees for 20 minutes or until golden brown. (Note: You may freeze for up to 3 months.)

MAKES 4 DOZEN

# Squash Casserole

1 pound squash, sliced
1/2 cup chopped onion
1/4 cup (1/2 stick) margarine
2 egg yolks, beaten
1 cup milk
10 (about) saltines, crushed

1 cup (4 ounces) shredded
  sharp Cheddar cheese
Salt to taste
1/4 teaspoon pepper
2 egg whites

Cook the squash in a small amount of water in a saucepan until tender; drain. Sauté the onion in the margarine in a skillet until translucent. Add the onion, egg yolks, milk, cracker crumbs, cheese, salt and pepper to the squash and mix well. Beat the egg whites at high speed in a mixing bowl until stiff peaks form. Fold into the squash mixture. Pour into a greased 8×8-inch baking dish. Bake at 350 degrees for 40 to 45 minutes or until set.

SERVES 4 TO 6

# Squash Supreme

2 cups mashed cooked squash
2 eggs, beaten
3/4 cup mayonnaise
10 green onions with
  tops, chopped
1/4 cup (1/2 stick) butter
  or margarine

1 cup (4 ounces) shredded
  Cheddar cheese
1 teaspoon salt
1 teaspoon pepper
1/2 cup crushed butter
  crackers

Sauté the green onions in the butter in a skillet until tender. Add the squash, eggs, mayonnaise, cheese, salt and pepper and mix well. Spoon into a buttered baking dish. Sprinkle with the cracker crumbs. Bake at 400 degrees for 25 to 30 minutes or until set.

SERVES 4 TO 6

# Zucchini Tomato Splash

3 zucchini
1 tomato, chopped
Chopped walnuts to taste
1 tablespoon butter

Cut the zucchini into thin slices. Sauté the zucchini, tomato and walnuts in the butter in a skillet for 10 minutes.

SERVES 4

# Sweet Potato Casserole

3 large sweet potatoes
3 large apples, peeled and sliced
1/2 cup chopped pecans
1/2 cup packed brown sugar
1 teaspoon cinnamon
1/2 cup (1 stick) butter

Boil the sweet potatoes in enough water to cover in a saucepan until tender; drain and cool. Peel the sweet potatoes and cut into slices. Layer 1/3 of the sweet potatoes, 1/3 of the apples, 1/4 cup of the pecans, the brown sugar and cinnamon in a baking dish. Continue to alternate the layers with the remaining sweet potatoes, apples and pecans. Slice the butter and place over the layers. Bake at 375 degrees for 30 minutes or until the apples are tender.

SERVES 8

# Sweet Potato Pudding

2 pounds sweet potatoes, roasted and peeled
3 eggs
1 cup heavy cream
Pinch of grated nutmeg
1/2 teaspoon cinnamon
1/2 cup pecan pieces
1/2 cup packed light brown sugar
2 tablespoons pure cane syrup
Pinch of salt
1/4 teaspoon vanilla extract
2 tablespoons bourbon
1/2 cup pecan pieces
1/2 cup packed light brown sugar
1/2 cup flour
1/2 cup flaked coconut
1/4 cup (1/2 stick) butter, softened

Mash the sweet potatoes in a mixing bowl until smooth. Stir in the eggs and cream. Add the nutmeg, cinnamon, 1/2 cup pecans, 1/2 cup brown sugar, syrup, salt, vanilla and bourbon and mix well. Spoon into a greased 1 1/2-quart round baking dish. Combine 1/2 cup pecans, 1/2 cup brown sugar, the flour, coconut and butter in a bowl and mix with your hands to form coarse crumbs. Spread over the sweet potato mixture. Bake at 350 degrees for 45 minutes or until bubbly.

SERVES 6

# Cranberry Casserole

3 cups chopped peeled apples
2 cups cranberries
1 (15-ounce) can pineapple tidbits, drained
1 cup pecans
3/4 cup packed brown sugar
3/4 cup sugar
1/3 cup flour
1/4 cup rolled oats
1/2 cup (1 stick) butter, melted

Combine the apples, cranberries, pineapple and pecans in a bowl and toss to mix. Spoon into a baking dish. Mix the brown sugar, sugar, flour and oats in a bowl. Spread over the cranberry mixture. Pour the butter over the top. Bake at 350 degrees for 30 minutes.

SERVES 8

# Scalloped Pineapple

4 cups fresh bread crumbs
1 (20-ounce) can pineapple chunks, drained
3 eggs, beaten
2 cups sugar
1 cup (2 sticks) butter, melted

SERVES 4 TO 6

Toss the bread crumbs and pineapple in a bowl. Place in a baking dish. Combine the eggs, sugar and butter in a bowl and mix well. Pour over the pineapple mixture. Bake at 350 degrees for 30 minutes.

# Crunchy Stuffed Eggs

6 hard-cooked eggs
1/4 cup sour cream
1/4 teaspoon salt
1/8 teaspoon pepper
1 teaspoon parsley
2 slices bacon, cooked and crumbled
Paprika to taste
6 pimento-stuffed olives, cut into halves

SERVES 12

Peel the eggs and cut into halves. Place the egg yolks in a bowl, reserving the egg white halves. Add the sour cream, salt, pepper and parsley to the egg yolks and mash until smooth. Stir in the bacon. Stuff into the egg whites. Sprinkle with paprika. Top each with an olive half.

## Macaroni and Cheese

4½ tablespoons butter
4½ tablespoons flour
3/8 teaspoon salt
Pepper to taste
1½ cups milk
1 pound Velveeta cheese, shredded
12 ounces macaroni, cooked and drained

Melt the butter in a saucepan. Stir in the flour, salt and pepper. Add the milk gradually, stirring constantly. Cook until blended, stirring constantly. Reserve 1 cup of the cheese. Add the remaining cheese gradually, stirring constantly. Cook until the cheese melts, stirring constantly. Add the macaroni and mix well. Spoon into a baking dish. Sprinkle with the reserved cheese. Bake at 325 degrees until the cheese melts and the top is brown.

SERVES 6 TO 8

## Fettuccini Special

2/3 cup freshly grated Parmesan cheese
½ cup (1 stick) butter, melted
1 cup heavy cream
1 cup sour cream
1 pound fettuccini, cooked and drained

Combine the cheese, butter, cream and sour cream in a bowl and mix well. Pour over the hot fettuccini in a large bowl and toss to coat.

SERVES 6

# Garlic Cheese Grits

3 1/2 quarts water
1 1/2 tablespoons salt
4 cups uncooked grits
5 garlic cloves, minced
2 pounds Velveeta cheese, cut into cubes
1 cup half-and-half
2/3 cup butter or margarine

SERVES 36

Bring the water and salt to a boil in a large Dutch oven. Stir in the grits and garlic gradually. Cover and reduce the heat. Simmer for 10 minutes, stirring occasionally. Add the cheese, half-and-half and butter. Simmer until the cheese and butter melt, stirring constantly.

# Dirty Rice

1 onion, chopped
1/2 cup (1 stick) margarine, melted
1 cup uncooked rice
1 (10-ounce) can beef consommé
1 (4-ounce) jar sliced mushrooms, drained
1 cup water

SERVES 4 TO 6

Sauté the onion in the margarine in a skillet. Add the rice. Sauté until the rice is light brown. Add the consommé, mushrooms and water and mix well. Spoon into a baking dish. Bake at 350 degrees for 40 minutes.

## Yellow Rice Casserole

1 large or 2 small packages yellow rice
1 (16-ounce) can whole kernel corn, drained
1 (10-ounce) can cream of mushroom soup
1 soup can water
1 1/2 cups (6 ounces) shredded cheese

Cook the rice using the package directions. Combine the rice, corn, soup, water and cheese in a bowl and mix well. Spoon into a baking dish. Bake at 350 degrees for 20 minutes or until bubbly.

SERVES 6 TO 8

## Rice Dressing

1 pound ground chuck
1 onion, chopped
1 bell pepper, chopped
1 (10-ounce) can cream of mushroom soup
1 (10-ounce) can cream of chicken soup
1 (10-ounce) can Cheddar cheese soup
1 cup cooked rice

Brown the ground chuck, onion and bell pepper in a skillet, stirring until the ground chuck is crumbly; drain. Combine the mushroom soup, chicken soup and Cheddar cheese soup in a bowl and mix well. Add to the ground chuck mixture and mix well. Stir in the rice. Spoon into a baking dish. Bake at 375 degrees for 30 minutes.

SERVES 6 TO 8

The George Bryan Reading Park was dedicated September 1, 2001, in honor of the retirement of George W. Bryan as vice president of the Sara Lee Corporation. This beautiful park features a center fountain with walkways leading to four corners with benches for relaxation and reading. In each of the four corners are bronze busts of some of the great Mississippi writers: William Faulkner, Richard Wright, Tennessee Williams, and Eudora Welty. George Bryan is married to Marcia L. Bryan and has three daughters, Suzanne Bryan Sampietro, Nancy B. Campbell, and Laura B. Williams, and one son, Wilkes Bryan. George also served as president of Bryan Foods, Inc., from 1974 to 1983. He is the son of the late John Bryan, Sr., founder of Bryan Foods, Inc.

# SOUPS & CONDIMENTS

## BACK TO NATURE

*Following the motto, "Care today, Character tomorrow," one of the biggest ways in which the West Point Junior Auxiliary reaches the children in our community is through our Child Welfare School project, Back to Nature. Back to Nature is a yearly project offered to the children who live in lower-income housing developments. The children range in age from five through ten. Every summer, the WPJA plans arts and crafts activities and games and provides snacks for the children. Through all activities, the WPJA emphasizes strong character and self-esteem development.*

# Turkey Gumbo

1 large onion, chopped
1 green bell pepper, chopped
1 large rib celery, chopped
2 large garlic cloves, crushed
2 tablespoons butter
2 turkey drumsticks, or 2½ pounds chicken
4 cups water
1 bay leaf
1 teaspoon salt
½ teaspoon thyme
¼ teaspoon pepper
1 (16-ounce) can tomatoes, broken up
1 (10-ounce) can sliced okra
Hot cooked white rice
Hot pepper sauce to taste

Sauté the onion, bell pepper, celery and garlic in the butter in a Dutch oven until tender. Add the turkey, water, bay leaf, salt, thyme and pepper. Bring to a boil. Cover and reduce the heat. Simmer for 1½ hours or until the turkey is tender. Remove the turkey. Chop the turkey, discarding the skin and bones. Return the chopped turkey to the Dutch oven. Add the tomatoes and okra. Simmer, covered, for 20 minutes or until the okra is tender. Discard the bay leaf. Ladle over the rice in individual soup bowls and season with hot pepper sauce.

SERVES 4 TO 6

# Corn Chowder

3 potatoes, chopped
1 onion, chopped
½ cup (1 stick) margarine
1 cup chicken broth or water
Minced garlic to taste
Salt and pepper to taste
1 (17-ounce) can niblet corn
1 (17-ounce) can cream-style corn
3 cups milk

Combine the potatoes, onion, margarine and broth in a large saucepan. Bring to a boil and reduce the heat to low. Boil until the potatoes are soft and most of the water has been absorbed. Add the garlic, salt and pepper. Stir in the niblet corn, cream-style corn and milk. Cook until of the desired consistency, adding additional milk if needed. Ladle into soup bowls. (Note: You may cook in a slow cooker for 6 hours or more.)

SERVES 4 TO 6

67

# Chicken Broccoli Soup

1 (10-ounce) package frozen chopped broccoli
3 cups chopped green onions
3 ribs celery, chopped
2 carrots, shredded
1/4 cup (1/2 stick) margarine
2 (10-ounce) cans chicken broth
3 (10-ounce) cans potato soup
Parsley flakes to taste
Salt and pepper to taste
Tabasco sauce to taste
3 tablespoons cooking sherry (optional)
1 cup sour cream
8 ounces Cheddar cheese, shredded
4 chicken breasts, cooked and chopped

Cook the broccoli using the package directions; drain. Sauté the green onions, celery and carrots in the margarine in a large saucepan. Add the chicken broth and potato soup. Simmer for 30 minutes. Stir in the parsley, salt, pepper, Tabasco sauce and cooking sherry. Add the sour cream and cheese. Cook for 15 minutes. Stir in the broccoli and chicken. Cook until heated through. Ladle into soup bowls. Serve with corn bread.

SERVES 8

# Cheesy Chicken Soup

1 cup finely chopped celery
1 cup finely chopped onion
1 cup finely chopped carrots
1 (16-ounce) package frozen
    mixed vegetables
4 cups chicken broth
3 cups chopped
    cooked chicken
1 pound mild Mexican
    Velveeta cheese, cut into
    cubes
2 (10-ounce) cans cream of
    chicken soup
Salt and pepper to taste

Cook the celery, onion, carrots and mixed vegetables in the chicken broth in a large saucepan until tender. Add the chicken, cheese, canned soup, salt and pepper and mix well. Cook until the cheese melts and the soup is heated through. Ladle into soup bowls.

SERVES 6 TO 8

# Grandpa's Chicken Noodle Soup

6 chicken breasts
8 cups water
2 tablespoons chicken
    bouillon granules
1 teaspoon basil
1 bay leaf
1/2 teaspoon salt
1/2 teaspoon pepper
2 cups chopped onions,
    carrots and celery
4 ounces egg noodles

Combine the chicken, water, bouillon granules, basil, bay leaf, salt and pepper in a large saucepan. Cook until the chicken is tender. Remove the chicken to a plate. Chop the chicken, discarding the skin and bones. Return the chicken to the saucepan. Add the vegetables. Bring to a boil. Add the noodles. Cook until the noodles are al dente. Discard the bay leaf. Ladle into soup bowls.

SERVES 6 TO 8

# Taco Soup

2 pounds ground beef
1 onion, chopped
3 (14-ounce) cans Mexican stewed tomatoes
1 envelope taco seasoning mix
1 envelope ranch salad dressing mix
1 (8-ounce) can Mexicorn
1 (11-ounce) can Shoe Peg corn
1 (15-ounce) can hot chili beans
1 (15-ounce) can ranch-style beans
1 (4-ounce) can chopped green chiles, drained

*B*rown the ground beef and onion in a skillet, stirring until the ground beef is crumbly; drain. Bring the stewed tomatoes to a boil in a large saucepan. Add the taco seasoning mix and ranch salad dressing mix. Boil for 10 to 12 minutes, stirring frequently. Add the ground beef mixture, Mexicorn, Shoe Peg corn, chili beans, ranch-style beans and green chiles and mix well. Simmer for 30 to 45 minutes. Ladle into soup bowls. Serve with corn chips and shredded cheese.

SERVES 8

# Shrimp and Corn Soup

½ cup (1 stick) butter
2 tablespoons flour
1 large onion, chopped
4 cups frozen corn
1 (10-ounce) can tomatoes with green chiles
2 pounds peeled medium shrimp
½ teaspoon thyme
½ teaspoon basil
1 cup water
1 tablespoon salt
1 tablespoon white pepper
½ cup chopped green onions
1 tablespoon parsley

Cook the butter and flour in a large saucepan over low heat to form a peanut-colored roux, stirring constantly. Add the onion. Sauté until translucent. Add the corn, tomatoes with green chiles, shrimp, thyme, basil, water, salt and white pepper. Simmer, uncovered, for 1 hour. Add the green onions and parsley. Simmer, uncovered, for 15 minutes, adding additional water if needed for the desired consistency. Ladle into soup bowls. (Note: You may use crawfish tails instead of shrimp.)

SERVES 4 TO 6

71

# Broccoli Cheese Soup

½ onion, chopped
Salt and pepper to taste
2 tablespoons butter
2 cups milk
2 (10-ounce) cans chicken broth

1 roll garlic cheese
1 roll jalapeño cheese
1 (16-ounce) package frozen
   chopped broccoli

**SERVES 8**

Sauté the onion, salt and pepper in the butter in a large saucepan until the onion is translucent. Add the milk, chicken broth, garlic cheese and jalapeño cheese and mix well. Stir in the broccoli. Simmer over low heat until the broccoli is tender. Ladle into soup bowls.

# Baked Potato Soup

6 large baking potatoes, baked
1 onion, chopped
1 cup (2 sticks) butter
1 cup flour
4 cups milk
1 (10-ounce) can chicken broth
2 cups half-and-half

1 pound sliced bacon, cooked
   and crumbled
1 pound Cheddar cheese,
   shredded
1 cup sour cream
4 green onions, chopped
Salt and pepper

**SERVES 8**

Peel the baked potatoes. Cut into slices. Sauté the onion in a nonstick skillet until translucent. Melt the butter in a large saucepan. Stir in the flour. Cook to form a blonde roux, stirring constantly. Add the milk gradually, stirring constantly. Add the sautéed onion, chicken broth, half-and-half, bacon and cheese and mix well. Stir in the potatoes, sour cream, green onions, salt and pepper. Simmer until heated through. Ladle into soup bowls. (Note: This soup is very thick. You can add additional milk or chicken broth or use a little less flour when making the roux for the desired consistency.)

# Spinach Tomato Tortellini Soup

2 tablespoons unsalted butter
6 to 8 garlic cloves, minced
4 cups chicken broth
6 ounces cheese tortellini
1 (14-ounce) can diced tomatoes

10 ounces fresh spinach, rinsed and coarsely chopped
8 to 10 fresh basil leaves, coarsely chopped
Grated Parmesan cheese to taste

Melt the butter in a large saucepan over medium heat. Add the garlic. Sauté for 2 minutes or until fragrant. Add the chicken broth. Bring to a boil. Add the pasta. Cook for 5 minutes. Add the undrained tomatoes and reduce the heat. Simmer until the pasta is tender. Stir in the spinach and basil. Cook for 1 to 2 minutes or until the spinach is wilted. Ladle into soup bowls. Sprinkle with Parmesan cheese.

SERVES 6 TO 8

# Coca-Cola Barbecue Sauce

1 cup coca-cola
1 cup ketchup
1/4 cup Worcestershire sauce
3 tablespoons A.1. steak sauce

1 teaspoon onion flakes
1 teaspoon garlic flakes
1/2 teaspoon freshly ground pepper

Combine the coca-cola, ketchup, Worcestershire sauce, steak sauce, onion flakes, garlic flakes and pepper in a heavy nonreactive saucepan. Bring to a boil gradually over medium heat and reduce the heat. Simmer for 6 to 8 minutes or until the sauce is reduced by a quarter. Use right away or pour into a large jar and cool to room temperature. Store, covered, in the refrigerator for several months.

MAKES 2 CUPS

73

# Blender Hollandaise Sauce

3 egg yolks
1 to 2 tablespoons lemon juice
¼ teaspoon salt
Dash of cayenne pepper
½ cup (1 stick) butter, melted

MAKES 1 CUP

*Blend* the egg yolks, lemon juice, salt and cayenne pepper at high speed in a blender. Add the melted butter gradually, processing constantly. (Note: The sauce will keep at room temperature for 1 hour before serving.)

# Cherry Sauce

¾ cup water
¼ cup sugar
½ cup packed brown sugar
1 teaspoon horseradish
1 teaspoon mustard
1 (14-ounce) can chopped Bing cherries

MAKES 1 TO 1½ CUPS

*Combine* the water, sugar and brown sugar in a saucepan. Cook over low heat until the sugar dissolves, stirring constantly. Add the horseradish, mustard and cherries and mix well. Cook until heated through. Serve with pork or chicken.

## Jezebel Sauce

1 (18-ounce) jar apple jelly
1 (18-ounce) jar pineapple preserves
3 tablespoons dry mustard
1/2 cup horseradish
1 tablespoon coarsely ground pepper

Combine the jelly, preserves, dry mustard, horseradish and pepper in a bowl and mix well. Store, covered, in the refrigerator for several weeks. Serve with pork or beef, or pour over cream cheese to serve as an appetizer.

MAKES 4 TO 4 1/2 CUPS

## Caesar Salad Dressing

1/2 cup vegetable oil
1/2 cup (2 ounces) grated Parmesan cheese
1/4 cup lemon juice
1 tablespoon Worcestershire sauce
1/2 teaspoon salt
1/2 teaspoon pepper
2 garlic cloves, minced

Combine the oil, Parmesan cheese, lemon juice, Worcestershire sauce, salt, pepper and garlic in a bowl and blend well. Serve over Caesar salad. (Note: You may substitute 1/2 cup canola oil and 1/2 cup olive oil for the vegetable oil.)

MAKES 1 CUP

75

# Honey Mustard Dressing

10 tablespoons honey
1 cup mayonnaise
3/4 cup mustard
1/4 tablespoon red pepper

MAKES 2 CUPS

Combine the honey, mayonnaise, mustard and red pepper in a bowl and mix well. Store in an airtight container in the refrigerator for several weeks.

# Orange Salad Dressing

1/4 cup orange juice
1/2 cup vegetable oil
2 tablespoons sugar
3 tablespoons cider vinegar
1 tablespoon lemon juice
1/4 teaspoon salt

Combine the orange juice, oil, sugar, vinegar, lemon juice and salt in a jar with a tight-fitting lid. Cover the jar and shake well to mix. Serve over mixed greens with mandarin oranges and walnuts.

MAKES ABOUT 1 CUP

# Sweet-and-Spicy Pickles

1 (1-gallon) jar dill pickle slices
6 cups sugar
1 cup cider vinegar
1 tablespoon pickling spice
2 teaspoons whole allspice
4 cinnamon sticks

Layer the pickles and sugar ⅓ at a time in a 1-gallon jar with a tight-fitting lid. Combine the vinegar, pickling spice, allspice and cinnamon sticks in a microwave-safe bowl and mix well. Microwave on High until the mixture boils. Pour over the pickles and secure with the lid. Store the pickles at room temperature for 48 hours or until the sugar dissolves, inverting the jar twice a day and storing upright. Store in the refrigerator. Serve chilled.

MAKES 1 GALLON

# Cranberry Relish

1 (6-ounce) package raspberry gelatin
1 cup boiling water
1 (16-ounce) can whole cranberry sauce
1 (16-ounce) can crushed pineapple
1 cup chopped nuts

Dissolve the gelatin in boiling water in a bowl. Stir in the cranberry sauce. Add the pineapple and nuts and mix well. Spoon into a serving dish. Chill until set.

SERVES 8

Located in the middle of town, KidTown found its beginnings as a tennis court. In 1994, a few mothers in town asked the city to turn it into a much-needed space for the small children of our community. They raised the money for equipment and paint...and KidTown was born. It serves as a place to host kid's parties and tons of fun.

But, by 2003, it had become run down. The West Point Junior Auxiliary recognized the need for refurbishment and decided to take the park as a much-needed project for the kids in our community.

# SALADS

## KIDTOWN

We began by asking for quotes for new asphalt and paint. A local contractor, Neal Coker with Falcon Contracting, donated the asphalt for the project. Local businesses let us purchase paint at cost and donated free supplies to help out. We designed the park to have bright, colorful games to play painted on the asphalt. Additionally, we purchased extra playground equipment. With the help of other local civic organizations, the grounds around the park were landscaped.

The playground is beautiful and boasts a sign on the fence that reads, "KidTown—Be nice or leave."

# Green Bean and Cherry Tomato Salad with Herb Dressing

1 1/2 pounds slender green beans,
trimmed and cut into 2-inch pieces
Salt to taste
3/4 cup chopped seeded tomatoes
1/3 cup extra-virgin olive oil
2 tablespoons balsamic vinegar
2 garlic cloves, minced
1 teaspoon oregano
Pepper to taste
1/4 cup chopped fresh Italian parsley
1 cup cherry tomato halves

Boil the green beans in enough salted water to cover in a saucepan for
3 minutes or until tender-crisp; drain. Plunge immediately into a bowl of
ice water to stop the cooking process; drain. Place the green beans in a
large bowl.

Combine the tomatoes, olive oil, vinegar, garlic and oregano in a bowl
and mix well. Add to the green beans and stir to mix well. Season with salt
and pepper. Sprinkle with the parsley and cherry tomatoes.

SERVES 8

## Broccoli Salad

2 heads broccoli, cut into florets
1 cup sunflower seeds
1 cup raisins
1 bunch green onions, chopped
1 cup mayonnaise
1/2 cup sugar
3 tablespoons vinegar
1 pound sliced bacon, cooked and crumbled

Combine the broccoli, sunflower seeds, raisins and green onions in a bowl and toss to mix. Blend the mayonnaise, sugar and vinegar in a small bowl. Add to the broccoli mixture and toss to coat. Sprinkle with the bacon just before serving.

SERVES 8

## Broccoli Salad with Ranch Dressing

1 head broccoli, cut into florets
1 bunch green onions, chopped
2 carrots, sliced
1 bell pepper, chopped
1 cup mayonnaise
1 envelope ranch salad
    dressing
Bacon bits to taste

Combine the broccoli, green onions, carrots and bell pepper in a bowl and toss to mix well. Blend the mayonnaise and salad dressing in a bowl. Add to the broccoli mixture and toss to coat. Marinate, covered, in the refrigerator for 1 hour or longer. Sprinkle with bacon bits just before serving.

SERVES 4 TO 6

81

# Twenty-Four-Hour Coleslaw

1 head cabbage, shredded
1 onion, sliced
3/4 cup sugar
1 cup vinegar
1 1/2 teaspoons salt

1 teaspoon celery seeds
1 teaspoon sugar
1 teaspoon dry mustard
3/4 cup vegetable oil

Alternate layers of the cabbage and onion in a large bowl. Sprinkle with 3/4 cup sugar. Combine the vinegar, salt, celery seeds, 1 teaspoon sugar and dry mustard in a small saucepan and mix well. Bring to a boil. Remove from the heat. Stir in the oil. Pour over the cabbage layers. Do not stir. Chill, covered, for 24 hours. Toss to mix when ready to serve.

SERVES 8

# Marinated Carrots

5 cups fresh carrots, peeled
and sliced
Salt to taste
3/4 cup vinegar
1/2 cup vegetable oil
1 (10-ounce) can
tomato bisque

1 cup sugar
1 teaspoon mustard
1 teaspoon pepper
1 teaspoon Worcestershire
sauce
1 onion, sliced
1 green bell pepper, sliced

Boil the carrots in salted water to cover in a saucepan until tender; drain. Place the carrots in a large bowl. Bring the vinegar, oil, tomato bisque, sugar, mustard, pepper and Worcestershire sauce to a boil in a saucepan. Add the onion and bell pepper. Pour over the carrots. Marinate, covered, in the refrigerator for 8 to 12 hours. Serve with a slotted spoon.

SERVES 10 TO 12

## Corn Salad

1 envelope zesty Italian salad dressing mix
1 cup ranch salad dressing
¼ teaspoon garlic powder
¼ cup red wine vinegar
1 cup cherry tomato halves
1 cucumber, peeled and chopped
2 (11-ounce) cans Shoe Peg corn
Bacon bits to taste
French-fried onions to taste

*B*lend the Italian salad dressing mix and ranch salad dressing in a bowl. Add the garlic powder and vinegar and blend well. Combine the tomatoes, cucumber and corn in a large bowl. Add the dressing mixture and mix well. Chill for 30 minutes. Sprinkle with bacon bits and French-fried onions before serving.

SERVES 8

## Black-Eyed Pea Salad

1 (16-ounce) can black-eyed peas, drained
1 onion, chopped
2 tomatoes, chopped
¼ cup sugar
1 small bottle fat-free Italian salad dressing

*C*ombine the black-eyed peas, onion, tomatoes and sugar in a bowl and mix well. Stir in the salad dressing. Chill, covered, before serving.

SERVES 4

# Eight-Layer Salad

12 slices bacon
1 head lettuce, rinsed and drained
1 cup chopped celery
1 (16-ounce) can green peas
½ cup chopped green bell pepper
1 red onion, chopped
2 cups mayonnaise
2 tablespoons sugar
1 cup (4 ounces) shredded Cheddar cheese

Fry the bacon in a skillet until crisp. Remove to paper towels to drain. Crumble the bacon. Tear the lettuce into bite-size pieces. Layer the lettuce, celery, green peas, bell pepper, onion and bacon in the order listed in a 9×13-inch glass dish. Combine the mayonnaise and sugar in a bowl and mix well. Spread over the layers. Sprinkle with the cheese. Chill, covered, for 8 to 12 hours.

SERVES 8

# Crunchy Romaine Toss

1 (3-ounce) package ramen noodles
1 cup walnuts, chopped
¼ cup (½ stick) unsalted butter
1 bunch broccoli, coarsely chopped
1 head romaine, rinsed and torn into pieces
4 green onions, chopped
1 cup Sweet-and-Sour Dressing (below)

Crumble the ramen noodles, discarding the seasoning packet. Brown the ramen noodles and walnuts in the butter in a skillet. Remove to paper towels to drain. Combine the ramen noodles, walnuts, broccoli, romaine and green onions in a salad bowl and toss to mix. Pour the Sweet-and-Sour Dressing over the salad and toss to coat.

SERVES 10 TO 12

# Sweet-and-Sour Dressing

1 cup vegetable oil
1 cup sugar
½ cup wine vinegar
1 tablespoon soy sauce
Salt and pepper to taste

Process the oil, sugar, vinegar, soy sauce, salt and pepper in a blender until blended.

MAKES 2½ CUPS

# Spinach Salad

½ cup olive oil
½ cup vegetable oil
5 tablespoons red wine vinegar
¼ cup sour cream
2 garlic cloves, crushed
½ teaspoon dry mustard
1 tablespoon sugar
2 teaspoons minced parsley
½ teaspoon salt
¼ teaspoon pepper
1 package fresh spinach, trimmed
6 fresh mushrooms, sliced
3 hard-cooked eggs, chopped
6 slices bacon, cooked and crumbled

SERVES 4

Combine the olive oil, vegetable oil, vinegar, sour cream, garlic, dry mustard, sugar, parsley, salt and pepper in a jar with a tight-fitting lid. Cover with the lid and shake to mix well. Store in the refrigerator. Combine the spinach and mushrooms in a serving bowl and toss to mix. Add the desired amount of dressing and toss to coat. Top with the eggs and bacon.

## Korean Spinach Salad

3/4 cup vegetable oil
1/4 cup vinegar
1/3 cup ketchup
1/4 cup sugar
1 tablespoon Worcestershire sauce
1 package fresh spinach, trimmed and torn into bite-size pieces

1 (8-ounce) can water chestnuts, drained and sliced
1 bunch scallions, chopped
3 or 4 hard-cooked eggs, chopped
6 to 8 slices bacon, cooked and crumbled

Combine the oil, vinegar, ketchup, sugar and Worcestershire sauce in a jar with a tight-fitting lid. Cover the jar with the lid and shake to mix well. Store in the refrigerator.

Mix the spinach, water chestnuts, scallions, hard-cooked eggs and bacon in a salad bowl. Add the desired amount of salad dressing and toss to coat.

SERVES 8

## Summer Squash Coleslaw

2 small yellow squash, julienned
2 small zucchini, julienned
1 red bell pepper, julienned
1/3 cup chopped onion
3 tablespoons vegetable oil
2 tablespoons cider vinegar or white wine vinegar

1/2 cup sugar
1 tablespoon mayonnaise
1/2 teaspoon dill weed
1/2 teaspoon garlic salt
1/4 teaspoon celery seeds
1/4 teaspoon pepper

Combine the squash, zucchini, bell pepper and onion in a large bowl. Mix the oil, vinegar, sugar, mayonnaise, dill weed, garlic salt, celery seeds and pepper in a small bowl. Pour over the squash mixture and toss to coat. Chill, covered, until ready to serve.

SERVES 4 TO 6

# Marinated Vegetable Salad

1/2 cup white vinegar
   1/2 cup sugar
1 tablespoon corn oil
   1 teaspoon water
   1 teaspoon salt
   1 teaspoon pepper
   1/2 teaspoon paprika
1 (16-ounce) can green peas,
   drained
1 (11-ounce) can Shoe Peg
   corn, drained

1 (16-ounce) can French-cut
   green beans, drained
1 (8-ounce) can sliced water
   chestnuts, drained
1 (2-ounce) jar chopped
   pimento, drained
1 onion, chopped
1/2 cup chopped green bell
   pepper

*Heat* the vinegar and sugar in a small saucepan until dissolved. Remove from the heat to cool. Add the oil, water, salt, pepper and paprika and mix well. Combine the green peas, corn, green beans, water chestnuts, pimento, onion and bell pepper in a bowl and mix well. Pour the vinegar mixture over the vegetables. Marinate, covered, in the refrigerator until ready to serve.

SERVES 8

# Sour Cream Fruit Salad

1 cup seedless red grapes
1 (11-ounce) can mandarin
   oranges, drained
1 cup shredded coconut

1 (15-ounce) can pineapple
   chunks, drained
1 cup miniature marshmallows
1 cup sour cream

*Combine* the grapes, mandarin oranges, coconut, pineapple and marshmallows in a bowl and toss to mix. Fold in the sour cream. Chill until serving time.

SERVES 4 TO 6

# Fruit Salad

1 (15-ounce) can pineapple tidbits
2 tablespoons flour
2 eggs, beaten
1 cup sugar
Juice of 2 lemons
3 Granny Smith apples, chopped
3 bananas, sliced
1 cup chopped pecans
Miniature marshmallows to taste

Drain the pineapple, reserving 1/2 cup of the juice. Combine the reserved pineapple juice, flour, eggs, sugar and lemon juice in a saucepan and mix well. Cook until thickened, stirring constantly. Chill in the refrigerator.

Combine the pineapple, apples, bananas, pecans and marshmallows in a bowl and toss to mix. Add the chilled dressing and toss to coat.

SERVES 4 TO 6

# Light Fruit Salad

1 cup orange juice
1 small package sugar-free vanilla instant pudding mix
1 (11-ounce) can mandarin oranges, drained
2 (8-ounce) cans pineapple chunks, drained
3 bananas, sliced

Whisk the orange juice and pudding mix in a bowl until smooth and thick. Add the mandarin oranges, pineapple and bananas and mix well. Chill for 30 minutes to 12 hours before serving. (Note: You may add fresh strawberries and blueberries.)

SERVES 6 TO 8

# Cherry Fruit Salad

16 ounces whipped topping
1 cup sour cream
1 (14-ounce) can sweetened
    condensed milk
1/4 cup lemon juice
1 (16-ounce) can sliced
    peaches, drained

1 (20-ounce) can crushed
    pineapple, drained
1 (11-ounce) can mandarin
    oranges, drained
1 (21-ounce) can cherry pie
    filling
1 jar maraschino cherries

Combine the whipped topping, sour cream, condensed milk and lemon juice in a large bowl and mix well. Stir in the peaches, pineapple, mandarin oranges, cherry pie filling and maraschino cherries. Chill, covered, until ready to serve.

SERVES 8 TO 10

# Bacon Mandarin Salad

1/2 cup olive oil
1/4 cup red wine vinegar
1/4 cup sugar
1 tablespoon chopped
    fresh basil
1/8 teaspoon hot sauce
2 (11-ounce) cans mandarin
    oranges, drained and chilled

1 bunch red leaf lettuce,
    rinsed and torn
1 head romaine, rinsed
    and torn
1 pound sliced bacon, cooked
    and crumbled
1 (4-ounce) package sliced
    almonds, toasted

Whisk the olive oil, vinegar, sugar, basil and hot sauce in a large bowl until well blended. Add the mandarin oranges, red leaf lettuce and romaine and toss gently to coat. Sprinkle with the crumbled bacon and toasted almonds. Serve immediately.

SERVES 12

90

# Mandarin Orange Salad

10 ounces whipped topping
1 (3-ounce) package orange gelatin
8 ounces small curd cottage cheese
1 (11-ounce) can mandarin oranges, drained

Combine the whipped topping and gelatin in a bowl and mix well. Stir in the cottage cheese and mandarin oranges. Spoon into a serving bowl. Chill until set.

SERVES 8

# Sunshine Salad

⅓ cup sugar
1 (3-ounce) package orange gelatin
1 cup boiling water
1 cup sour cream
1 (8-ounce) can crushed pineapple
1 (11-ounce) can mandarin oranges, drained

Dissolve the sugar and gelatin in the boiling water in a large bowl. Add the sour cream and beat until blended. Stir in the undrained pineapple and mandarin oranges. Spoon into a salad mold. Chill until set. Unmold onto a serving plate to serve.

SERVES 8

# Strawberry Sour Cream Salad

1 (6-ounce) package strawberry gelatin
1 cup boiling water
1 (10-ounce) package frozen strawberries
1 (8-ounce) can crushed pineapple
½ cup chopped pecans
1½ cups sour cream

Dissolve the gelatin in the boiling water in a bowl. Add the strawberries, undrained pineapple and pecans and mix well. Pour ½ of the strawberry mixture into a 9×13-inch dish. Chill for 2 hours or until set. Spread the sour cream over the congealed layer. Pour the remaining strawberry mixture over the top. Chill until firm.

SERVES 12

# Hollywood Vine Salad

1 head romaine, rinsed and torn
2 hearts of palm, cut up
6 pitted green olives
6 pitted black olives
Pepperoni slices to taste
2 hard-cooked eggs, cut up
Grated Parmesan cheese to taste
Crumbled blue cheese to taste
Favorite salad dressing to taste

Combine the romaine, hearts of palm, green olives, black olives, pepperoni, eggs, Parmesan cheese and blue cheese in a large salad bowl and toss to mix. Add the salad dressing and toss to coat.

SERVES 2

92

# Chicken Salad

2 cups finely chopped cooked chicken breasts
1 cup chopped celery
2 hard-cooked eggs, grated
½ teaspoon salt
½ teaspoon pepper
1 tablespoon lemon juice
¾ cup chopped toasted pecans
3 or 4 slices bacon, cooked and crumbled
¾ cup mayonnaise

Combine the chicken, celery, eggs, salt, pepper, lemon juice, pecans, bacon and mayonnaise in a large bowl and mix well. Chill, covered, for 4 to 5 hours before serving. Garnish with paprika or chopped fresh parsley. Serve with thinly sliced rye bread.

SERVES 8

# Turkey Salad

1½ cups mayonnaise-type salad dressing or mayonnaise
¼ cup lemon juice
1 teaspoon salt
Pepper to taste
½ cup sugar
1 onion, chopped
7 ounces macaroni or bow tie pasta, cooked and drained
3 cups chopped cooked turkey
1 carrot, grated
1 cup chopped celery
½ cup sliced radishes
½ cup chopped green bell pepper
1 cup (4 ounces) shredded cheese or cubed cheese

Process the salad dressing, lemon juice, salt, pepper, sugar and onion in a blender. Combine the pasta, turkey, carrot, celery, radishes, bell pepper and cheese in a large bowl and mix well. Add the dressing and mix well. (Note: You may prepare a day ahead and store in the refrigerator. You may add or omit any fresh vegetables as you like.)

SERVES 8

# Tuna Salad

1 (9-ounce) can tuna, drained
6 ounces cream cheese, softened
2 ribs celery, chopped
4 hard-cooked eggs, chopped
Sweet pickle relish to taste
Chopped pecans to taste

SERVES 8

Combine the tuna, cream cheese, celery, eggs, relish and pecans in a bowl and mix well. Serve on croissants or with crackers.

# Crab Meat Pasta Salad

2 (8-ounce) packages imitation crab meat, chopped
1 rib celery, chopped
1 large onion, chopped
1/4 cup (1/2 stick) butter or vegetable oil
8 ounces spaghetti, cooked and drained
Salt to taste
Cayenne pepper to taste
Grated Parmesan cheese to taste

SERVES 8

Sauté the crab meat, celery and onion in the butter in a large skillet. Add the pasta and toss to mix. Season with salt, cayenne pepper and Parmesan cheese.

# Perfect Pasta Salad Toss

8 ounces penne, cooked and drained
4 ounces pepperoni, chopped
1 (7-ounce) jar roasted red peppers, drained and chopped
1 (6-ounce) jar marinated artichoke hearts, drained
½ cup pitted black olives
⅓ cup pitted green olives
2 teaspoons basil
1 cup (4 ounces) mixed cheeses
½ cup Italian or Caesar salad dressing

Combine the pasta, pepperoni, red peppers, artichoke hearts, black olives, green olives, basil and cheeses in a large bowl and toss to mix well. Add the salad dressing and toss to coat. Chill, covered, for 30 minutes or up to 6 hours. Serve on salad plates lined with romaine. (Note: This recipe can easily be doubled.)

SERVES 4 TO 6

# Crisp Macaroni Salad

2 cups shell macaroni, cooked,
   drained and cooled
1½ cups thinly sliced celery
½ cup chopped green
   bell pepper
½ cup chopped onion
¼ cup drained pickle relish

1 cup Cheddar cheese cubes
2 hard-cooked eggs
½ cup mayonnaise
½ cup sour cream
1 to 2 teaspoons salt
¼ cup chopped pimentos

Combine the macaroni, celery, bell pepper, onion, relish, cheese and eggs in a large bowl and toss to mix. Blend the mayonnaise, sour cream and salt in a small bowl. Pour over the macaroni mixture and toss to coat. Stir in the pimentos. Chill, covered, until ready to serve.

SERVES 4

# Spaghetti Salad

8 ounces vermicelli
1 (8-ounce) bottle zesty
   Italian salad dressing
1 envelope Italian salad
   dressing mix
½ (3-ounce) jar Salad
   Supreme seasoning

½ green bell pepper, chopped
½ purple onion, chopped
1 (2-ounce) can sliced black
   olives, drained

Cook the pasta using the package directions; drain. Add the salad dressing, salad dressing mix, Salad Supreme seasoning, bell pepper, onion and black olives and toss to mix. Spoon into a large bowl. Chill, covered, until ready to serve. (Note: You may store for up to 10 days in the refrigerator.)

SERVES 8

# Wild Rice and Cranberry Salad

1 (6-ounce) package long grain and wild rice mix
1 cup sweetened dried cranberries
1 cup chopped broccoli florets
4 green onions, chopped
3 ribs celery, thinly sliced
1 (2-ounce) jar chopped pimento, drained
1/2 cup Sweet-and-Sour Dressing (below)
1 cup dry-roasted peanuts

Prepare the wild rice mix using the package directions. Remove from the heat to cool. Spoon into a large bowl. Add the cranberries, broccoli, green onions, celery and pimento and mix well. Stir in the Sweet-and-Sour Dressing gently. Chill, covered, for at least 2 hours. Stir in the peanuts just before serving.

SERVES 6 TO 8

## Sweet-and-Sour Dressing

1/2 cup vegetable oil
1/2 cup sugar
1/4 cup wine vinegar
2 teaspoons soy sauce
Salt and pepper to taste

Combine the oil, sugar, vinegar, soy sauce, salt and pepper in a bowl and blend well.

MAKES 1 CUP

The beautiful Catherine "Kitty" Bryan Dill Memorial Parkway, a rail to trails project, was given in memory and honor of one of West Point's "favorite" ladies by her family, Mayor Kenny Dill, Mary Margaret Dill Case, Ken Dill, Jr., Caroline Billups, and Sarah Catherine Reily. Kitty Dill, 1942-1990, was the daughter of Mr. and Mrs. John Bryan, Sr. John Bryan was one of the founders of Bryan Foods, Inc. Kitty lived her entire life in West Point and believed in the community and being involved in the nurturing of West Point. Her memory lives on through the Parkway.

# CHICKEN
# BEEF
# PORK

## ADOPT A FAMILY

Each year, the West Point Junior Auxiliary adopts two or three families for the year. We work with the Department of Human Services and other social service organizations in West Point as a starting point to find our families. We then interview several families to hear firsthand what their struggles and their areas of need are. After two or three families are selected, the WPJA assists these families with purchasing school clothes and basic necessities monthly, such as toothpaste, soap, etc. Additionally, we provide Thanksgiving dinner, Easter baskets, and Valentine's candy. Our favorite event we do for our families is Christmas shopping. We ask the parents of our families for wish lists, and several WPJA members take these lists and go shopping. Other members wrap the gifts, and a few days before Christmas, Santa comes to their homes. It is a joy to see the happiness one can bring to a home with a little financial help.

# Almond-Crusted Chicken

3/4 cup dry bread crumbs

Coarse salt and freshly ground pepper to taste

1 1/2 cups sliced almonds, broken into pieces

2 eggs

2 teaspoons water

2 whole boneless skinless chicken breasts

2 tablespoons unsalted butter

2 tablespoons canola oil

Season the bread crumbs with salt and pepper in a medium bowl and toss to mix. Place the almonds in a bowl. Beat the eggs and water lightly in a small bowl. Dip the chicken in the egg mixture, wiping away the excess with your fingers. Dredge in the seasoned bread crumbs until lightly coated. Dip in the egg mixture again. Coat thoroughly with the almonds.

Heat the butter and oil in a 12-inch ovenproof skillet over medium heat. Add the chicken. Cook for 3 minutes or until brown. Turn the chicken. Cook for 1 minute longer. Bake at 400 degrees for 10 minutes or until the chicken is cooked through.

SERVES 4

## Buttermilk Chicken

3/4 cup flour
1/2 teaspoon salt
1/4 teaspoon pepper
4 to 6 skinless chicken breasts
1/2 cup buttermilk
1/4 cup (1/2 stick) margarine
1 cup buttermilk
1 (10-ounce) can cream of mushroom soup

Mix the flour, salt and pepper together. Dip the chicken in 1/2 cup buttermilk. Roll in the flour mixture to coat. Melt the margarine in a 9x13-inch baking pan. Place the chicken breast side down in the margarine. Bake at 425 degrees for 45 minutes. Turn the chicken. Bake for 30 minutes longer. Turn the chicken again. Mix 1 cup buttermilk and the soup in a bowl. Pour over the chicken. Bake for 30 minutes or until the chicken is cooked through. Remove the chicken to a platter. Garnish with parsley. Serve with the pan gravy.

SERVES 4 TO 6

# Chicken Fajitas

1/2 cup lime juice
1/4 cup vegetable oil
2 garlic cloves, finely chopped
1/2 teaspoon black pepper
1/4 teaspoon crushed red pepper
1/4 teaspoon salt
6 boneless skinless chicken breasts, cut into strips
1 tablespoon vegetable oil
12 tortillas

Combine the lime juice, 1/4 cup oil, garlic, black pepper, red pepper and salt in a bowl and mix well. Place the chicken in a shallow dish. Pour the marinade over the chicken. Marinate, covered, in the refrigerator for 2 hours. Drain the chicken, discarding the marinade. Sauté the chicken in 1 tablespoon oil in a skillet until cooked through. Spoon into warm tortillas. (Note: You may sauté chopped onion and green bell pepper slices with the chicken.)

SERVES 6

# Italian Chicken

1 whole chicken, cut up
1 envelope Italian salad dressing mix
1 (10-ounce) can cream of mushroom soup
1 onion, chopped
6 ounces cream cheese, cut into cubes
1/2 cup white cooking wine

Place the chicken in a slow cooker. Sprinkle with the salad dressing mix. Cook on High for 6 to 8 hours or until cooked through. Combine the soup, onion, cream cheese and wine in a small saucepan. Heat until the cream cheese melts, stirring constantly. Pour over the chicken. Cook on High for 30 minutes.

SERVES 4 TO 6

# Moroccan Chicken

1 (3- to 3 1/2-pound) frying chicken, cut up and skinned
1 1/4 cups chicken broth
1/2 cup golden raisins
1/2 teaspoon cinnamon
1/2 teaspoon turmeric
1 large onion, chopped
1 small package baby carrots
2 tablespoons flour

*B*rown the chicken in a skillet sprayed with nonstick cooking spray over medium-high heat. Add 1 cup of the chicken broth, the raisins, cinnamon, turmeric, onion and carrots. Bring to a boil and reduce the heat. Simmer, covered, for 15 to 20 minutes or until the chicken is tender and the juices run clear. Remove the chicken and vegetables to a serving platter, reserving the liquid in the skillet.

Combine the remaining 1/4 cup chicken broth and the flour in a jar with a tight-fitting lid. Cover the jar and shake well. Add to the reserved liquid in the skillet, stirring constantly. Cook until thickened and bubbly, stirring constantly. Pour over the chicken and vegetables. Serve with hot cooked rice.

SERVES 6

# Chicken Pasta Parmesan

1 pound boneless skinless chicken breasts
2 tablespoons vegetable oil
1 cup sliced mushrooms
1/4 cup chopped onion
2 tablespoons dry sherry
1 (10-ounce) can cream of chicken soup
1/2 cup thinly sliced red or green bell peppers
1/2 cup (2 ounces) grated Parmesan cheese

SERVES 2

Brown the chicken in the oil in a skillet. Remove the chicken to a platter, reserving the drippings in the skillet. Add the mushrooms and onion to the reserved drippings in the skillet. Sauté until the onion is tender. Add the sherry and soup. Cook until heated through, stirring frequently. Return the chicken to the skillet. Add the bell peppers. Simmer, covered, for 10 minutes or until the chicken is cooked through. Stir in the Parmesan cheese. Heat until melted. Serve over hot cooked pasta.

# Skillet Turkey Steaks Parmesan

1 pound turkey breast steaks, 3/8 to 1/2 inch thick
1½ teaspoons lemon juice
2 tablespoons flour
1 teaspoon salt
⅛ teaspoon pepper
1 egg
1 tablespoon water
½ cup seasoned bread crumbs
½ cup (2 ounces) shaved or grated Parmesan cheese
2 tablespoons butter
2 tablespoons vegetable oil

*Drizzle* the turkey with the lemon juice. Mix the flour, salt and pepper together. Beat the egg and the water in a bowl. Mix the bread crumbs and Parmesan cheese in a shallow dish. Dip the turkey in the seasoned flour and shake off the excess. Dip in the egg mixture, allowing the excess to drip off. Roll in the bread crumb mixture.

Heat the butter and oil in a large heavy skillet. Add the turkey. Cook for 2 minutes on each side or until well browned and the juices run clear. Garnish with lemon slices and sprigs of fresh basil.

SERVES 2

# Sweet-and-Sour Chicken

1 onion, finely chopped
1 small green bell pepper, cut into strips
2 tablespoons butter
2 tablespoons brown sugar
1 tablespoon Tabasco sauce
1 tablespoon Worcestershire sauce
1 teaspoon salt
3/4 cup ketchup
2 broiler chickens, quartered

SERVES 8

Sauté the onion and bell pepper in the butter in a saucepan over low heat until the onion is tender. Add the brown sugar, Tabasco sauce, Worcestershire sauce, salt and ketchup and mix well. Simmer for 10 minutes. Place the chickens on a rack in a roasting pan. Brush with some of the sauce. Bake at 350 degrees for 50 minutes or until the chicken is cooked through, basting frequently with the remaining sauce. Serve over hot fluffy white rice.

# One-Pot Chicken and Sausage

8 ounces Italian sausage links, cut diagonally into thirds
4 skinless chicken breasts (2½ pounds)
2 teaspoons olive oil
3 garlic cloves, chopped
1 teaspoon rosemary
1 pound unpeeled small red potatoes, cut into quarters
3 tablespoons water
½ teaspoon salt
¼ teaspoon pepper
¼ cup dry white wine
3 tablespoons balsamic vinegar
2 small red bell peppers, cut into 1-inch squares

*B*rown the sausage in a nonstick skillet for 8 minutes. Remove to a platter. Place the chicken breast side down in the drippings in the skillet. Cook for 5 minutes, turning once. Remove to the plate with the sausage.

Heat the olive oil in a skillet. Add the garlic and rosemary. Sauté for 1 minute. Add the potatoes and water. Cook, covered, for 15 minutes. Push the potatoes to the side of the skillet. Return the chicken and sausage to the skillet. Stir in the salt, pepper, wine, vinegar and bell peppers. Cook, covered, over medium-low heat for 35 minutes or until the chicken juices run clear. Remove the chicken and sausage to a platter and cover. Cover the skillet. Cook for 8 minutes or until the potatoes are tender. Pour over the chicken and sausage.

SERVES 4

# White Chili

4 or 5 chicken breasts
1 onion, chopped
6 (15-ounce) cans white
    Northern beans
1 (11-ounce) can tomatoes
    with green chiles
1 (15-ounce) can crushed tomatoes
1 teaspoon salt
1 teaspoon pepper
Tortilla chips to taste
Shredded cheese to taste

Cook the chicken in enough water to cover in a large saucepan until tender. Remove the chicken to a platter, reserving the broth. Chop the chicken, discarding the skin and bones. Combine the chicken, onion, reserved broth, beans, tomatoes with green chiles, crushed tomatoes, salt and pepper in a slow cooker. Cook on High until of the desired consistency. Ladle into chili bowls. Sprinkle with tortilla chips and cheese.

SERVES 8

# Chili

2½ to 3 pounds ground round
2 (28-ounce) cans diced tomatoes
1 tomato can water
3 (16-ounce) cans light red kidney beans, drained
1 large bell pepper, chopped
4 garlic cloves, chopped
1 large sweet onion, chopped
1 tablespoon basil
1 tablespoon parsley
2 tablespoons cumin
5 tablespoons beef bouillon granules
3 tablespoons chili powder
Salt and cracked pepper to taste
Hot sauce to taste

*B*rown the ground round in a skillet, stirring until crumbly; drain. Combine the ground round, tomatoes, water, beans, bell pepper, garlic, onion, basil, parsley, cumin, bouillon granules, chili powder, salt, pepper and hot sauce in a large saucepan and mix well. Cook for 1 hour or until of the desired consistency.

SERVES 8 TO 10

109

# Beef Tips

2 round steaks, cut into bite-size pieces
1 (10-ounce) can golden mushroom soup
1 (10-ounce) can cream of chicken soup
1 envelope onion soup mix

Place the beef in a slow cooker. Pour the mushroom soup and chicken soup over the beef. Sprinkle with the onion soup mix. Cook on Low for 6 hours. Serve over hot cooked rice or noodles. (Note: You may use stew beef if desired.)

SERVES 6 TO 8

## Saucy Beef over Rice

2 tablespoons flour
1 (14-ounce) can stewed tomatoes
1 envelope onion soup mix
1/2 cup water
1/2 teaspoon pepper
1 pound beef sirloin steak, cut into thin strips
2 cups hot cooked rice

Place the flour in an oven cooking bag and shake well. Place in a 9×13-inch baking pan. Add the undrained tomatoes, soup mix, water and pepper to the bag. Squeeze the bag to blend the ingredients. Add the beef to the bag, turning the bag to coat the beef. Arrange the ingredients in an even layer. Close the bag with the nylon tie and cut six 1/2-inch slits in the top of the bag. Bake at 350 degrees for 40 to 45 minutes or until the beef is tender. Spoon over the hot rice.

SERVES 4

# Chinese Beef and Beans

2 envelopes brown gravy mix
1 teaspoon sugar
1/4 teaspoon ginger
1 pound round steak, cut into
    thin strips
2 tablespoons soy sauce
1 to 2 tablespoons vegetable oil
2 (15-ounce) cans French-
    style green beans
1 1/3 cups water

Mix the gravy mix, sugar and ginger in a bowl. Combine with the round steak in a bowl and stir until coated. Add the soy sauce and stir until coated. Heat 1/2 of the oil in a skillet. Add the green beans. Cook for 5 minutes. Place in a 9×13-inch dish. Heat the remaining oil in the skillet. Add the steak. Cook for 3 to 5 minutes or until no longer pink, stirring constantly. Return the green beans to the skillet. Stir in the water. Cook until heated through, stirring constantly. Serve over hot cooked rice.

SERVES 6 TO 8

# Shanghai Beef

1 pound round steak,
    cut into thin strips
2 tablespoons vegetable oil
2 tablespoons cornstarch
1 1/2 cups beef broth
5 scallions, cut up
1 (8-ounce) can sliced water
    chestnuts, drained
3 tablespoons soy sauce
1/4 teaspoon pepper
1 1/2 cups uncooked
    instant rice

Sauté the beef in the oil in a large skillet for 5 minutes or until brown. Add the cornstarch and blend well. Add the beef broth, scallions, water chestnuts, soy sauce and pepper. Bring to a full boil, stirring frequently. Stir in the rice. Cover and remove from the heat. Let stand for 5 minutes. Fluff with a fork and serve.

SERVES 4

111

# London Broil

3 pounds London broil
4 teaspoons meat tenderizer
2 tablespoons sugar
1/4 cup Worcestershire sauce

1/4 cup sherry
2 tablespoons honey
2 teaspoons salt

Pierce the beef with a fork. Place in a shallow dish. Mix the meat tenderizer, sugar, Worcestershire sauce, sherry, honey and salt in a bowl. Pour over the beef. Marinate, covered, in the refrigerator for 6 hours, turning frequently to marinate both sides. Drain the beef, reserving the marinade. Boil the reserved marinade in a saucepan for 3 minutes. Place the beef on a grill rack. Grill over hot coals for 7 to 9 minutes on each side or until the desired doneness, basting with the cooked reserved marinade. Do not overcook.

SERVES 6

# Pot Roast with Tomatoes and Green Chiles

1 (2- to 4-pound) English shoulder roast
Flour for dredging
2 garlic cloves, minced
Olive oil for sautéing

1 (10-ounce) can chicken broth
1 (11-ounce) can tomatoes with green chiles
1/3 bottle good red wine

Dredge the roast in the flour. Sauté the garlic in the olive oil in a Dutch oven. Add the roast. Cook until the roast is seared on both sides. Add the chicken broth, tomatoes with green chiles and red wine. Simmer for 3 to 4 hours or until the roast is tender.

SERVES 6 TO 8

# Slow-Cooker Beef Roast

1 beef roast
Minced garlic to taste
Pepper to taste
1/4 cup soy sauce
1/4 cup Worcestershire sauce
1/2 teaspoon sugar
1 teaspoon liquid smoke
1 teaspoon hot sauce
1 tablespoon chopped onion

Rub the roast with garlic and pepper. Place in a sealable plastic bag. Combine the soy sauce, Worcestershire sauce, sugar, liquid smoke, hot sauce and onion in a bowl and mix well. Pour over the roast and seal the bag. Marinate in the refrigerator for 8 to 12 hours. Place the beef and marinade in a slow cooker. Cook on High for 8 to 12 hours or until the beef is tender.

SERVES 8

# Bacon-Wrapped Pork Tenderloin

2 pork tenderloins, cut into halves
8 slices bacon
1 (8-ounce) bottle Russian salad dressing

Wrap 2 bacon slices around each tenderloin half and secure with wooden picks. Place in a baking dish. Pour the salad dressing over the top. Marinate, covered, in the refrigerator for 24 hours. Bake, uncovered, at 350 degrees for 1 hour or until the pork is cooked through.

SERVES 4

The Everson-Wise Drainage project was awarded the
Best Public Facility Project with the Governor's Committee
of Excellence Award to the City of West Point in 2003.
This lake and fountain enhances the beauty of the newly
completed south parkway area. In the Kitty Bryan Dill Parkway,
the fountain overlooks a gazebo. This beautiful fountain
is lighted at night and is a spectacular sight to view
as you walk through the parkway.

# SEAFOOD & GAME BIRDS

## STUFF THE VAN

*Reaching out to all school-aged children in our community is the main mission of the Child Welfare Schools projects of the Junior Auxiliary. For many years, the West Point Junior Auxiliary has collected and distributed school supplies to all schools in the area. For the past two years, the "Stuff the Van" project has been developed in collaboration with Wal-Mart and Mitchell Automotive. This project is a highly publicized, one-day school supply drive held at our local Wal-Mart in which local citizens are asked to help stuff a minivan with school supplies and uniforms. Because our local school district has recently mandated uniforms, this regulation has become a new need for the children in our community, but "Stuff the Van" has helped WPJA meet this new challenge. Many more children have been helped with such massive community support.*

# Sautéed Shrimp with Grits and Cream Sauce

1½ pounds large shrimp
Cavender's Greek seasoning to taste
Lemon juice for sprinkling
¾ cup (1½ sticks) butter
1 tablespoon flour

1 green onion, finely chopped
6 tablespoons white wine vinegar
¾ cup heavy cream
Grits (below)

SERVES 4 TO 6

Peel and devein the shrimp. Place in a large bowl. Add the Greek seasoning and lemon juice and toss to coat. Melt the butter in a large heavy skillet. Add the shrimp. Sauté until the shrimp turn pink. Remove the shrimp to a bowl using a slotted spoon, reserving the liquid in the skillet. Blend the flour into the reserved liquid. Whisk in the green onion and vinegar. Whisk in the cream gradually. Heat until the cream is fully incorporated into the sauce, whisking constantly. Spoon the Grits onto serving plates. Arrange the shrimp over the grits. Spoon the sauce over the top.

## Grits

2½ cups chicken broth
1 tablespoon butter
¾ cup quick-cooking grits
3 tablespoons cream cheese

2 tablespoons half-and-half or cream
½ cup finely chopped green onions

Bring the chicken broth and butter to a boil in a saucepan. Stir in the grits. Simmer, covered, for 5 minutes. Stir in the cream cheese and half-and-half. Simmer, covered, for 7 minutes or until almost all of the liquid has evaporated. Stir in the green onions. Remove from the heat.

# Final Four Champagne Shrimp

1 pound medium shrimp, peeled and deveined
2 cups heavy cream
1/2 cup Champagne or dry white wine
1 (4-ounce) jar whole mushrooms, drained
3 tablespoons minced shallots or chives
1/4 teaspoon salt
1/3 cup chopped red bell pepper
1 teaspoon flour
Hot cooked capellini
Freshly cracked pepper to taste

*B*ring the shrimp, cream and Champagne to a boil in a large skillet over high heat. Boil until the shrimp turn pink. Remove the shrimp with a slotted spoon to a bowl, reserving the liquid in the skillet. Reduce the heat to medium-high. Boil the reserved liquid for 15 to 17 minutes or until the mixture is reduced to 1 1/4 cups. The mixture will be thick, bubbly and pale yellow in color. Reduce the heat to low. Add the shrimp, mushrooms, shallots and salt to the reduced sauce. Toss the bell pepper with the flour. Add to the shrimp mixture. Simmer for 2 to 3 minutes or until the shrimp are heated through. Spoon over hot cooked capellini. Sprinkle with pepper.

SERVES 4 TO 6

117

# Barbecued Shrimp

2 cups (4 sticks) butter
5 pounds fresh shrimp,
    peeled and deveined
5 garlic cloves, minced
5 tablespoons Worcestershire
    sauce

2 or 3 tablespoons Tabasco
    sauce
Juice of 1 lemon
Salt and pepper to taste

*Melt* the butter in a large heavy skillet. Add the shrimp, garlic, Worcestershire sauce, Tabasco sauce, lemon juice, salt and pepper. Sauté over low heat for 30 to 45 minutes or until the shrimp turn pink. Serve with crusty French bread.

SERVES 8 TO 10

## Spicy Barbecued Shrimp

6¼ pounds unpeeled medium
    fresh shrimp
½ cup (1 stick) butter or
    margarine, melted
¼ cup Worcestershire sauce
1 tablespoon Old Bay
    seasoning

¼ cup lemon juice
1 tablespoon coarsely ground
    pepper
1 or 2 garlic cloves, minced
1 tablespoon Cajun seasoning
1 tablespoon hot sauce

*Peel* and devein the shrimp. Combine the shrimp, butter, Worcestershire sauce, Old Bay seasoning, lemon juice, pepper, garlic, Cajun seasoning and hot sauce in a lightly greased large shallow roasting pan and toss to coat. Arrange the shrimp in a single layer. Bake at 350 degrees for 15 to 20 minutes or until the shrimp turn pink, stirring occasionally. (Note: You may peel and devein the shrimp a day ahead and store in a sealable plastic bag in the refrigerator.)

SERVES 12

# Cajun Seafood Pasta

1 pound fettuccini, linguini or other pasta
3/4 cup (1 1/2 sticks) butter
6 tablespoons flour
1 tablespoon salt
6 cups milk
3 tablespoons grated Parmesan cheese
1/2 cup (1 stick) butter
3 garlic cloves, minced
1 (8-ounce) package imitation crab meat
1 pound shrimp, peeled and deveined
1/2 teaspoon wine or sherry
2 teaspoons Cajun seasoning
Dash of oregano leaves
Salt and pepper to taste

Cook the pasta using the package directions. Melt 3/4 cup butter in a saucepan. Stir in the flour and salt. Stir in the milk gradually. Cook until thickened, stirring constantly. Stir in the Parmesan cheese. Melt 1/2 cup butter in a large stockpot. Add the garlic, crab meat, shrimp, wine, Cajun seasoning, oregano leaves, salt and pepper. Sauté to separate the crab meat and until the shrimp turn pink. Add the sauce and mix well. Drain the hot pasta. Add to the shrimp mixture and toss to coat. Cook until heated through. The sauce will thicken.

SERVES 7 OR 8

119

# Sautéed Crayfish over Pasta

½ cup (1 stick) butter
1 tablespoon white wine Worcestershire sauce
1½ teaspoons Creole seasoning
1 garlic clove, minced
8 ounces mushrooms, thinly sliced
1 pound crayfish, peeled
¼ cup chopped green onion tops
1 tablespoon flour
8 ounces cream cheese or ricotta cheese
2 cups half-and-half, warmed
⅓ cup freshly grated Parmesan cheese
Hot cooked pasta

SERVES 4

Melt the butter in a skillet. Add the wine Worcestershire sauce, Creole seasoning, garlic and mushrooms. Sauté until the mushrooms are tender. Add the crayfish and green onion tops. Sauté for 3 to 5 minutes or until the crayfish are cooked through. Add the flour and stir until smooth. Stir in the cream cheese and half-and-half. Heat until the cream cheese melts. Stir in the Parmesan cheese. Spoon over hot cooked pasta.

## Crawfish Fettuccini

1 onion, chopped
2 tablespoons butter
1 (10-ounce) can cream of mushroom soup
1 (10-ounce) can cream of celery soup
1 small jar jalapeño Cheez Whiz
1 pound crawfish tails or shrimp, peeled
8 ounces fettuccini, cooked and drained

Sauté the onion in the butter in a stockpot. Add the mushroom soup, celery soup and Cheez Whiz and mix well. Add the undrained crawfish tails. Cook until the crawfish tails are cooked through. Add the hot cooked fettuccini and toss to coat.

SERVES 4

121

# Gourmet Doves

24 dove breasts
Cavender's Greek seasoning
    to taste
Salt and pepper to taste
4 green onion tops, chopped
4 garlic cloves, minced

8 ounces button mushrooms,
    sliced
1/4 cup (1/2 stick) butter
1/4 cup extra-virgin olive oil
1 (10-ounce) can beef consommé
1 cup red wine

Remove the breasts from the bones. Sprinkle the breasts with Greek seasoning, salt and pepper. Sauté the green onions, garlic and mushrooms in the butter and olive oil in a skillet until tender. Add the dove breasts. Cook until tender. Do not overcook. Add the consommé and red wine. Cook until the sauce is reduced and thickened. (Note: You may thicken the sauce with cornstarch if you plan to serve over white rice.)

SERVES 8 TO 10

# Dove Breasts

Flour for coating
Salt and pepper to taste
12 to 24 dove breasts
1/2 cup (1 stick) margarine
1 1/2 cups chopped celery

3/4 cup chopped onions
1 (6-ounce) can mushrooms,
    drained
1 (10-ounce) can chicken
    broth

Season the flour with salt and pepper. Dredge the dove breasts in the flour mixture to coat. Melt the margarine in a large saucepan. Add the dove breasts. Cook until brown. Remove the dove breasts to a platter, reserving the drippings in the saucepan. Add the celery and onions to the reserved drippings. Sauté until the onion is translucent. Stir in the mushrooms. Return the dove breasts to the saucepan. Add the chicken broth. Simmer, covered, for 3 hours, adding additional broth if necessary. Serve over wild rice.

SERVES 4 TO 8

# Roasted Pheasant

2 pheasants, skinned and quartered
Flour for coating
Vegetable oil for browning
Butter for browning
1 onion, thinly sliced
1 (10-ounce) can chicken noodle soup, or 1 cup chicken broth
1/2 cup sherry or sauterne

Coat the pheasant with flour. Heat an equal amount of oil and butter in a skillet to cover the bottom. Add the pheasant. Cook until brown. Remove to a 9×11-inch baking pan, reserving the drippings in the skillet. Add the onion to the reserved drippings. Sauté until translucent. Add the soup and sherry. Cook until heated through. Pour over the pheasant. Bake, covered, at 325 degrees for 2 to 2½ hours. Serve with hot cooked noodles or wild rice. Garnish with chopped fresh parsley. (Note: You may add sliced fresh mushrooms to the sauce. If the pheasant becomes dry, add additional chicken broth. This recipe is easily doubled.)

SERVES 4

123

The George Bryan Reading Park is the location of the bronze bust of one of Mississippi's great female writers, Eudora Welty. Her image evokes a profound respect and admiration for this Pulitzer Prize Winner's accomplishments as a literary author and beloved Mississippian. One could gaze into her eyes and think of her words, "I am a writer who came of a sheltered life. A sheltered life can be a daring life as well. For all serious daring starts from within."

# MAIN DISH CASSEROLES

## MENTORING

*Pens for Friends is a project for which each member of our chapter writes to a child every month. During the school year, they exchange greetings and stories about their families and friends. At the end of the school year, the WPJA organizes a party in which the pen pals can reveal their identities to each other. The WPJA hopes this positive experience will somehow encourage the girls to learn respect for and trust in others.*

# Chicken Casserole

4 large boneless skinless chicken breasts
1 chicken bouillon cube
1 tablespoon minced onion
Salt and pepper to taste
1 cup sour cream
1 (10-ounce) can cream of chicken soup
1 (10-ounce) can cream of celery soup
1 (8-ounce) can water chestnuts, drained
1 sleeve butter crackers
1 (4-ounce) jar sliced mushrooms, drained
1 cup (4 ounces) shredded Cheddar cheese
2 teaspoons poppy seeds
3/4 cup (1 1/2 sticks) butter or margarine, melted

Boil the chicken, bouillon cube, onion, salt and pepper in enough water to cover in a saucepan until the chicken is cooked through; drain. Cool the chicken and cut into small pieces. Mix the sour cream, chicken soup and celery soup in a bowl. Add the water chestnuts, mushrooms and chicken and mix well. Line a greased baking dish with whole butter crackers. Crumble the remaining butter crackers. Spoon the chicken mixture over the crackers. Sprinkle with the cheese, crumbled crackers and poppy seeds. Drizzle with the butter. Bake at 400 degrees until heated through and bubbly.

SERVES 4 TO 6

# Chicken Broccoli Casserole

1 (5-ounce) package yellow rice
½ whole chicken or 3 chicken breasts, cooked
1 (10-ounce) package frozen chopped broccoli, thawed
1 (10-ounce) can cream of mushroom soup
1 (10-ounce) can cream of chicken soup
½ cup mayonnaise
1 tablespoon lemon juice
Salt and pepper to taste
6 to 10 ounces Cheddar cheese, shredded

Cook the yellow rice using the package directions. Chop the chicken, discarding the skin and bones. Spread the broccoli in a 9×13-inch baking dish. Layer the rice and chicken over the broccoli. Mix the mushroom soup, chicken soup, mayonnaise, lemon juice, salt and pepper in a bowl. Spread over the layers. Sprinkle with the cheese. Bake at 325 degrees for 30 minutes. (Note: You can also stir the chicken and part of the cheese into the soup mixture.)

SERVES 8

127

# Company Chicken

1 small jar dried beef
10 boneless skinless chicken breasts
10 bacon slices
2 cups sour cream
2 (10-ounce) cans cream of chicken soup
3 ounces cream cheese, softened

*Line* a baking dish with the dried beef. Wrap each chicken breast with a bacon slice. Place over the dried beef. Mix the sour cream, soup and cream cheese in a bowl until smooth. Pour over the chicken. Cover with foil. Bake at 325 degrees for 2 hours. Uncover and continue to bake until light brown.

SERVES 10

# Chicken Cornflake Casserole

2 cups chopped cooked chicken
1 cup chopped celery
1/2 cup chopped onion
1 cup cooked rice
1 (10-ounce) can cream of chicken soup
1 (4-ounce) jar sliced mushrooms, drained
1/4 cup mayonnaise
1 tablespoon lemon juice
2 cups cornflakes
3 tablespoons butter, melted

*Combine* the chicken, celery, onion, rice, soup, mushrooms, mayonnaise and lemon juice in a bowl and mix well. Spoon into a nonstick baking dish. Toss the cornflakes with the butter in a bowl. Sprinkle over the chicken mixture. Bake at 350 degrees for 30 minutes.

SERVES 8

128

# Sour Cream Chicken Enchiladas

2 (10-ounce) cans cream of chicken soup
½ cup chopped onion
1 (4-ounce) can chopped green chiles, drained
1 cup sour cream
½ teaspoon salt
1 package flour tortillas
4 or 5 chicken breasts, cooked and shredded
2 cups (8 ounces) shredded Monterey Jack cheese

Combine the soup, onion, green chiles, sour cream and salt in a saucepan. Heat until the mixture is warm, stirring frequently. Do not boil. Spoon a small amount of the mixture into a 9×12-inch baking dish. Fill each tortilla with the chicken, some of the remaining sauce and some of the cheese. Roll up to enclose the filling. Arrange in the prepared dish. Top with the remaining sauce and cheese. Bake at 350 degrees for 30 minutes.

SERVES 8

129

# Greek Chicken Spaghetti

6 chicken breasts
Salt to taste
1 large onion, chopped
1 large bell pepper, chopped
½ cup (1 stick) margarine
1 (4-ounce) can sliced black olives, drained
1 (28-ounce) can tomatoes, chopped
1 (4-ounce) jar mushrooms, drained
2 cups chicken broth
2½ tablespoons Greek seasoning
8 ounces feta cheese, crumbled
1 cup (4 ounces) shredded sharp Cheddar cheese
1 pound spaghetti, cooked and drained

Cook the chicken in enough salted water to cover in a saucepan until cooked through; drain. Chop the chicken, discarding the skin and bones. Sauté the onion and bell pepper in the margarine in a skillet until the onion is translucent. Combine the chicken, sautéed vegetables, olives, undrained tomatoes, mushrooms, chicken broth and Greek seasoning in a large bowl and mix well. Add the feta cheese, Cheddar cheese and spaghetti and toss to mix well. Adjust the seasonings to taste and add additional broth if needed. Spoon into a large baking dish. Bake at 375 degrees for 20 to 30 minutes or until heated through.

SERVES 8

# King Ranch Chicken

1 onion, chopped
1 green bell pepper, chopped
¼ cup (½ stick) butter
1 (10-ounce) can cream of mushroom soup
1 (10-ounce) can cream of chicken soup
2 (11-ounce) cans tomatoes with green chiles
2 cups chopped cooked chicken
12 tortillas, torn into bite-size pieces
2 cups (8 ounces) shredded Cheddar cheese

Sauté the onion and bell pepper in the butter in a skillet until the onion is translucent. Add the mushroom soup, chicken soup, tomatoes with green chiles and chicken and mix well. Alternate layers of the chicken mixture, tortillas and cheese in a large baking dish until all ingredients are used. Bake at 325 degrees for 40 minutes.

SERVES 8

# Herbed Chicken

4 to 8 boneless skinless chicken breasts
1 cup (4 ounces) shredded Swiss cheese
1 (10-ounce) can cream of chicken soup
   ½ cup white wine
2 cups herb stuffing, coarsely crushed
   ½ cup (1 stick) butter, melted

SERVES 4 TO 8

*P*lace the chicken in a shallow baking dish. Sprinkle the chicken with the cheese. Mix the soup and wine in a bowl until smooth. Pour over the chicken. Top with the stuffing. Drizzle with the butter. Bake, uncovered, at 350 degrees for 1½ hours or until the chicken is cooked through.

# Slow-Baked Mexican Chicken

1¼ cups orange juice
1¼ cups grapefruit juice
   ½ cup water
   ¼ cup fresh lemon juice
   ½ cup chili powder or adobo paste
1 (4-pound) chicken, cut up and skin removed, or
2 pounds boneless skinless chicken breasts

*P*rocess the orange juice, grapefruit juice, water, lemon juice and chili powder in a blender for 1 minute. Layer the chicken in a large baking dish. Pour the juice mixture over the chicken. Marinate, covered, in the refrigerator for 24 hours.

Remove the chicken from the refrigerator and cover with foil. Bake at 300 degrees for 3 hours or until the chicken is cooked through. Remove from the oven. Let stand, covered, for 20 minutes. Skim the surface before serving.

SERVES 8

# Chicken Noodle Casserole

3 or 4 small boneless skinless chicken breasts
2/3 package egg noodles
2 (10-ounce) cans cream of chicken soup
1 soup can milk
1/4 cup (1/2 stick) butter, melted
3 slices Velveeta cheese
Salt and pepper to taste
1 sleeve butter crackers, crushed

Boil the chicken in enough water to cover in a saucepan for 40 minutes or until cooked through. Drain and cool. Cut the chicken into bite-size pieces. Cook the noodles using the package directions; drain. Mix the soup, milk and butter in a large bowl until smooth. Add the chicken, noodles and cheese and stir to mix well. Season with salt and pepper. Spoon into a large baking dish sprayed with nonstick cooking spray. Sprinkle with the crushed crackers. Bake at 350 degrees for 30 to 40 minutes or until bubbly in the middle.

SERVES 8

133

# Oriental Chicken Casserole

2 cups chopped        ½ cup chopped onion
  cooked chicken        1 (2-ounce) jar chopped
1 (3- to 5-ounce) can          pimento, drained
  chow mein noodles        1 (10-ounce) can cream of
1 (3-ounce) can chopped          chicken soup
  mushrooms, drained        ¾ cup mayonnaise
1 cup chopped celery

### SERVES 8

Combine the chicken, noodles, mushrooms, celery, onion and pimento in a bowl and mix well. Stir in a mixture of the soup and mayonnaise. Spoon into a buttered 9x13-inch baking dish. Bake at 350 degrees for 30 minutes.

# Chicken Pie

1 (3-pound) chicken        2 teaspoons baking powder
Salt to taste        1 teaspoon salt
1½ cups chicken broth        ½ teaspoon pepper
1 (10-ounce) can cream of        1 cup milk
  chicken soup        ½ cup (1 stick) margarine,
1 cup flour          melted

Boil the chicken in enough salted water to cover in a saucepan until cooked through; drain and cool. Cut the chicken into bite-size pieces, discarding the skin and bones. Place the chicken in a large baking dish. Mix the chicken broth and soup in a bowl. Pour over the chicken. Combine the flour, baking powder, 1 teaspoon salt and pepper in a bowl and mix well. Add the milk and margarine and mix well. Pour over the top. Bake at 425 degrees for 35 to 40 minutes or until golden brown.

### SERVES 8

# Festivities Poppy Seed
# Chicken Casserole

6 boneless skinless chicken breasts, cooked
Salt and pepper to taste
2 (10-ounce) cans cream of chicken soup
1/4 cup water
1 cup sour cream
8 ounces Monterey Jack cheese, shredded
3 tablespoons poppy seeds
2 sleeves butter crackers, crushed
3/4 cup (1 1/2 sticks) margarine, melted

Cut the chicken into strips. Arrange in a large baking dish. Season with salt and pepper. Cook the soup and water in a small saucepan over medium heat until smooth, stirring frequently. Remove from the heat. Stir in the sour cream. Add the cheese and 1 1/2 tablespoons of the poppy seeds. Pour over the chicken. Mix the crackers, remaining poppy seeds and margarine in a bowl. Sprinkle over the layers. Bake at 350 degrees for 30 minutes.

SERVES 8

135

# Hot Chicken Salad Casserole

4 cups chopped cooked chicken, chilled
2 tablespoons lemon juice
3/4 cup mayonnaise
1 teaspoon salt
1 cup chopped celery
4 hard-cooked eggs, chopped
1 (10-ounce) can cream of chicken soup
1 tablespoon minced onion
2 tablespoons chopped pimento
1 cup (4 ounces) shredded Cheddar cheese
1 1/2 cups crushed potato chips
2/3 cup finely chopped almonds

Combine the chicken, lemon juice, mayonnaise, salt, celery, eggs, soup, onion and pimento in a large bowl and mix well. Spoon into a 9x13-inch baking dish. Chill, covered, for 8 to 12 hours. Remove from the refrigerator and uncover. Sprinkle with the cheese, potato chips and almonds. Bake, uncovered, at 400 degrees for 30 minutes.

**SERVES 8**

# Chicken and Wild Rice Casserole

1 (6-ounce) package quick-cooking long grain
   and wild rice mix
½ cup (1 stick) butter
1 small onion, chopped
½ cup flour
1½ cups chicken broth
3 cups chopped cooked chicken
1½ cups half-and-half
1 (6-ounce) can sliced water chestnuts, drained
1 (4-ounce) jar sliced mushrooms, drained
1 tablespoon chopped fresh parsley
1 teaspoon salt
½ teaspoon pepper
1 (2-ounce) package sliced almonds

Cook the rice using the package directions. Melt the butter in a large skillet over medium-high heat. Add the onion. Sauté until tender. Add the flour. Cook for 1 minute, stirring constantly. Add the chicken broth. Cook for 1 to 2 minutes or until thickened and bubbly, stirring constantly. Stir in the rice, chicken, half-and-half, water chestnuts, mushrooms, parsley, salt and pepper. Spoon into a lightly greased 7×11-inch baking dish. Sprinkle with the almonds. Bake at 350 degrees for 15 to 20 minutes or until heated through.

SERVES 6

# Swedish Chicken

½ (10-ounce) can cream of    1 large jar dried beef
   celery soup             12 boneless skinless chicken
2 cups sour cream          breasts

Mix the soup and sour cream in a bowl. Spray a 9×13-inch baking dish
with nonstick cooking spray. Reserve 12 slices of the dried beef. Line the
dish with the remaining dried beef. Wrap each chicken breast in a slice of
the reserved dried beef. Place seam side down in the prepared dish. Pour
the soup mixture over the chicken. Bake, uncovered, at 350 degrees for
1 to 1½ hours or until the chicken is cooked through. Garnish with
candied apple slices.

SERVES 12

# He-Man Casserole

2 pounds round steak,    ½ cup chopped celery
   trimmed and cut into       (optional)
   ½-inch cubes              1 cup sour cream
3 tablespoons vegetable oil   1 (10-ounce) can tomato soup
1 large onion, chopped      1 tablespoon Worcestershire
1 garlic clove, minced         sauce
   2 tablespoons flour       ⅛ teaspoon pepper
1 (4-ounce) can broiled
   mushrooms with broth

Brown the steak in the oil in a skillet over medium heat. Add the onion
and garlic. Cook until golden brown. Remove from the heat. Stir in the
flour. Add the mushrooms, celery, sour cream, tomato soup, Worcestershire
sauce and pepper and mix well. Pour into a greased baking dish. Bake,
uncovered, at 325 degrees for 1 hour. Cover and bake for 30 minutes
longer. Serve over hot cooked rice or egg noodles.

SERVES 4

# Enchiladas

1 pound ground round
1 envelope taco seasoning mix
1 pound Jimmy Dean chili
2 (15-ounce) cans chili without beans
15 corn tortillas
1 onion, chopped
1 large package shredded Mexican cheese

*B*rown the ground round in a skillet, stirring until crumbly. Add the taco seasoning mix and prepare using the envelope directions.

Heat the chili and chili without beans in a saucepan over low to medium heat until heated through. Heat a tortilla on an oiled griddle. Spoon some of the ground round mixture, chili mixture, onion and cheese in the center. Roll up to enclose the filling. Place in a large baking dish. Repeat the process with the remaining tortillas. Add the remaining ground round mixture and a small amount of water to the remaining chili mixture. Pour over the tortilla roll-ups. Bake at 350 degrees until bubbly in the center. Sprinkle with the remaining cheese. Bake until the cheese melts. Serve with sour cream, jalapeño chiles and saltine crackers. (Note: Jimmy Dean chili comes in a roll like bulk pork sausage.)

SERVES 15

# Taco Casserole

1 pound ground beef
1 cup salsa
½ cup mayonnaise
2 teaspoons chili powder
2 cups crushed tortilla chips
1 cup (4 ounces) shredded Colby cheese
1 cup (4 ounces) shredded Monterey Jack cheese

*Brown* the ground beef in a skillet, stirring until crumbly; drain. Add the salsa, mayonnaise and chili powder and mix well. Spoon into a shallow baking dish. Layer the chips, Colby cheese and Monterey Jack cheese over the ground beef mixture. Bake at 350 degrees for 20 to 25 minutes or until heated through. Serve with lettuce, tomato and sour cream. (Note: You may add one 15-ounce can red beans or whole kernel corn.)

SERVES 4

# Mexican Stuffed Shells

  1 pound ground beef
  1 (8-ounce) can tomato sauce
  1/2 cup water
  1 (12-ounce) jar picante sauce
  8 ounces Monterey Jack Jalapeño Pepper cheese, shredded
  1 (3-ounce) can French-fried onions
  15 to 20 jumbo shells, cooked and drained

*B*rown the ground beef in a skillet, stirring until crumbly. Combine the tomato sauce, water, 1/2 of the picante sauce, 1/2 of the cheese and 1/2 of the French-fried onions in a bowl and mix well. Stir into the ground beef mixture. Stuff the mixture into the shells. Place in a large baking dish. Pour the remaining picante sauce over the stuffed shells. Bake, covered, at 350 degrees for 30 minutes. Uncover and sprinkle with the remaining cheese and remaining French-fried onions. Bake, uncovered, for 5 minutes.

SERVES 4

# Ground Beef Pie

1 pound ground beef
2 tablespoons butter or margarine
⅓ cup chopped onion
1 teaspoon salt
Dash of pepper
Dash of garlic powder
¼ cup chopped green bell pepper
1 (15-ounce) can peas and carrots
2 beef bouillon cubes
1 cup chopped cooked potato (optional)
⅓ cup flour
2 refrigerator pie pastries

Brown the ground beef in the butter in a large skillet over medium heat, stirring until crumbly; drain. Add the onion, salt, pepper, garlic powder and bell pepper. Cook until heated through. Add the undrained peas and carrots, bouillon cubes and potato. Cook until the bouillon cubes dissolve. Stir in the flour. Cook until thickened, stirring constantly. Fit 1 pie pastry into a pie plate. Pour the ground beef mixture into the prepared pie plate. Top with the remaining pie pastry, trimming and fluting the edge. Bake at 400 degrees for 20 to 25 minutes or until golden brown. Serve with broiled peaches.

SERVES 6

# Ground Beef Supreme

1½ pounds ground beef
1 (15-ounce) can whole tomatoes
1 (10-ounce) can pizza sauce
2 garlic cloves, minced
8 ounces medium egg noodles
1 cup sour cream
6 ounces cream cheese, cut into small cubes
6 green onions with tops, chopped

*B*rown the ground beef in a large skillet, stirring until crumbly; drain. Add the undrained tomatoes, pizza sauce and garlic. Simmer, uncovered, for 10 minutes. Prepare the noodles using the package directions; drain. Combine the noodles, sour cream, cream cheese and green onions in a bowl and mix well. Layer the noodle mixture and ground beef mixture ½ at a time in a greased 8×12-inch baking dish. Bake, covered, at 350 degrees for 35 minutes.

SERVES 6 TO 8

# Manicotti Casserole

2 pounds ground beef
1 (32-ounce) jar spaghetti sauce
1½ cups water
1 (12-ounce) package frozen spinach soufflé, thawed
12 ounces mozzarella cheese, shredded
8 ounces uncooked manicotti

*B*rown the ground beef in a skillet, stirring until crumbly; drain. Heat the spaghetti sauce in a large saucepan. Add the ground beef and water and mix well. Spoon some of the ground beef mixture into a 9×13-inch baking dish. Mix the spinach soufflé and cheese in a bowl. Stuff into the uncooked manicotti. Place the stuffed manicotti in the prepared dish. Cover with the remaining ground beef mixture. Cover tightly with foil. Bake at 350 degrees for 1 hour. Let stand for 15 minutes before serving.

SERVES 6 TO 8

# Pork Chop Casserole

3/4 cup uncooked rice
4 pork chops
1 onion, sliced
1 tomato, sliced
1 green bell pepper, sliced
1 (10-ounce) can beef broth

*Place* the uncooked rice in a baking dish. Brown the pork chops in a nonstick skillet. Arrange over the rice. Place the onion, tomato and bell pepper on top of each pork chop. Pour the beef broth over the top. Bake, covered, at 350 degrees for 1 hour.

SERVES 4

## Sausage Casserole

1 pound sausage
1 (10-ounce) can cream of mushroom soup
1 (10-ounce) can cream of chicken soup
1 (10-ounce) can Cheddar cheese soup
1/2 onion, chopped
2 soup cans water
1 cup uncooked rice

*Brown* the sausage in a skillet, stirring until crumbly; drain. Combine the mushroom soup, chicken soup, cheese soup, onion, water and uncooked rice in a bowl and mix well. Stir in the sausage. Spoon into a 9×13-inch baking dish. Bake at 350 degrees for 1 1/4 hours.

SERVES 8

# Sausage Spinach Lasagna

1 (5-link) package Italian sausage, casings removed
2 (32-ounce) jars spaghetti sauce
1 (10-ounce) package frozen chopped spinach,
   cooked and drained
72 ounces cottage cheese
3 eggs
1/4 cup chopped fresh parsley
Salt and pepper to taste
1 pound lasagna noodles, cooked
8 cups (32 ounces) shredded mozzarella cheese
1 cup (4 ounces) grated Parmesan cheese

Brown the sausage in a skillet, stirring until crumbly; drain. Add the spaghetti sauce and cooked spinach and mix well. Simmer until heated through. Mix the cottage cheese, eggs, parsley, salt and pepper in a bowl. Layer the noodles, sausage mixture, cottage cheese mixture, mozzarella cheese and Parmesan cheese 1/2 at a time in two foil baking pans. Bake at 350 degrees for 1 hour.

SERVES 16

145

# Cajun Crab Meat Pie

1 unbaked (8-inch) deep-dish pie shell
⅓ cup chopped green bell pepper
⅓ cup chopped celery
⅓ cup chopped onion
¼ cup (½ stick) margarine
2 eggs, beaten
1 cup half-and-half or cream
¾ teaspoon salt
½ teaspoon red pepper
1 cup (4 ounces) shredded Cheddar cheese
1 tablespoon flour
1 (6-ounce) can crab meat

Bake the pie shell at 450 degrees for 10 minutes. Remove from the oven and reduce the oven temperature to 325 degrees. Sauté the celery, onion and bell pepper in the margarine in a skillet until tender. Combine the eggs, half-and-half, salt and red pepper in a bowl and beat well. Stir in the sautéed vegetables. Mix the cheese, flour and crab meat in a bowl. Sprinkle into the prebaked pie shell. Pour the vegetable mixture over the top. Bake for 45 to 60 minutes or until a knife inserted in the center comes out clean. Garnish with finely chopped green onions. (Note: You may substitute shrimp for the crab meat.)

SERVES 6

146

# Artichoke and Shrimp Casserole

1 (14-ounce) can artichoke hearts
1 pound medium shrimp, cooked, peeled and deveined
4 ounces fresh mushrooms, sliced
2 tablespoons butter
4½ tablespoons butter
4½ tablespoons flour
1½ cups half-and-half
1 tablespoon Worcestershire sauce
¼ cup dry sherry
Salt and pepper to taste
¼ cup (1 ounce) grated Parmesan cheese
Paprika to taste

Drain the artichoke hearts. Cut into quarters and arrange in a buttered 1-quart baking dish. Pat the shrimp dry. Place the shrimp over the artichokes. Sauté the mushrooms in 2 tablespoons butter in a skillet for 6 minutes. Spoon over the shrimp. Melt 4½ tablespoons butter in a saucepan over low heat. Stir in the flour. Cook for 3 to 5 minutes, stirring constantly. Stir in the half-and-half gradually. Cook until thickened, stirring constantly. Stir in the Worcestershire sauce and sherry. Season with salt and pepper. Pour over the layers. Sprinkle with the Parmesan cheese and paprika. Bake at 375 degrees for 20 minutes. Garnish with chopped fresh parsley just before serving.

SERVES 6

147

# Delicious Shrimp Casserole

1 cup chopped onion
1 cup chopped bell pepper
1 cup chopped celery
3 garlic cloves, minced
1/2 cup (1 stick) margarine
2 (10-ounce) cans cream of mushroom soup
1 (10-ounce) can Cheddar cheese soup
1/3 cup parsley
1 cup chopped green onions
1 cup chopped cooked shrimp
1 (2-ounce) jar pimento, drained
2 cups cooked wild rice
1/2 cup Italian bread crumbs
2 tablespoons hot sauce
1 teaspoon salt
3/4 teaspoon pepper

Sauté the onion, bell pepper, celery and garlic in the margarine in a skillet until tender. Add the mushroom soup, cheese soup, parsley and green onions and mix well. Stir in the shrimp and pimento gently. Stir in the rice and bread crumbs. Season with hot sauce, salt and pepper. Spoon into a baking dish. Bake at 350 degrees for 30 minutes.

SERVES 4 TO 6

# Herbed Feta Shrimp

2 eggs
1 cup evaporated milk
1 cup yogurt
8 ounces feta cheese, crumbled
8 ounces Swiss cheese, shredded
1/2 cup chopped fresh parsley
1 teaspoon basil
1 teaspoon oregano
4 garlic cloves, minced
9 ounces angel hair pasta, cooked
1 (16-ounce) jar mild chunky salsa
2 pounds uncooked shrimp, peeled
8 ounces mozzarella cheese, shredded

Combine the eggs, evaporated milk, yogurt, feta cheese, Swiss cheese, parsley, basil, oregano and garlic in a bowl and mix well. Spread 1/2 of the pasta in an 8x12-inch baking dish coated with nonstick cooking spray. Cover with the salsa. Layer 1/2 of the shrimp, the remaining pasta, cheese mixture and remaining shrimp over the salsa. Sprinkle with the mozzarella cheese. Bake at 350 degrees for 30 minutes. Remove from the oven. Let stand for 10 minutes before serving.

SERVES 12

The Mann-Friday House was constructed in 1869 by Jabez Mann. His descendants owned and lived in the home for 120 years. The city of West Point purchased the house in 1998 to use as a permanent museum. The house displays artifacts of general community history, special displays of "Howlin' Wolf" memorabilia, and the history of Payne Field. It also features special exhibits throughout the year.

# CHOCOLATE!
# CHOCOLATE!
# CHOCOLATE!

## YOU ARE UNIQUE

*Every year, West Point Junior Auxiliary hosts a seminar at the local schools encouraging youth to wait until marriage to have sex. It also explains the dangers of sexually transmitted diseases, the emotional traumas of having sex before marriage, and the consequences of teenage pregnancy. It encourages youth to respect themselves and their parents.*

# Mississippi Mud Cake

1 cup (2 sticks) salted
  butter, melted
2 cups sugar
1½ cups sifted flour
½ cup baking cocoa
¼ teaspoon salt

1 cup pecans, chopped
4 eggs, beaten
2 teaspoons vanilla extract
1 (7-ounce) jar marshmallow
  creme
Chocolate Frosting (below)

Combine the butter, sugar, flour, baking cocoa, salt and pecans in a large mixing bowl and mix well. Add the eggs and vanilla and mix well. Spoon into a greased 9x15-inch cake pan. Bake at 350 degrees for 35 minutes. Remove from the oven. Spread with the marshmallow creme. Spread Chocolate Frosting over the top.

**SERVES 15**

## Chocolate Frosting

¼ cup (½ stick) butter
½ cup baking cocoa
1 (5-ounce) can evaporated milk
1 (1-pound) package confectioners' sugar

Melt the butter in a saucepan. Stir in the baking cocoa. Combine the cocoa mixture, evaporated milk and confectioners' sugar in a mixing bowl and beat until smooth.

# Chocolate Pound Cake

3 cups flour
1/2 teaspoon baking powder
1/2 cup baking cocoa
1 cup (2 sticks) butter, softened
1/2 cup shortening
3 cups sugar
5 eggs
1 1/4 cups milk
1 teaspoon vanilla extract

Mix the flour, baking powder and baking cocoa together. Cream the butter, shortening and sugar in a mixing bowl until light and fluffy. Add the eggs 1 at a time, beating well after each addition. Add the flour mixture and milk alternately, beating well after each addition. Stir in the vanilla. Spoon into a greased and floured tube or bundt pan. Bake at 325 degrees for 1 3/4 hours. Cool completely before removing from the pan. (Note: You can also bake in 3 greased and floured 5×7-inch loaf pans and store in the freezer to give as gifts.)

SERVES 16

# Chocolate Cookie Sheet Cake

1 cup water | 1/2 teaspoon salt
1/2 cup shortening | 2 eggs
3 tablespoons baking cocoa | 1/2 cup buttermilk
1/2 cup (1 stick) margarine | 1 teaspoon baking soda
2 cups flour | 1 teaspoon vanilla extract
2 cups sugar | Chocolate Icing (below)

SERVES 18 TO 20

Bring the water, shortening, baking cocoa and margarine to a boil in a saucepan, stirring constantly. Sift the flour, sugar and salt into a bowl. Add the eggs, buttermilk, baking soda and vanilla and mix well. Add the chocolate mixture and mix well. Pour into a greased sheet cake pan. Bake at 350 degrees for 20 minutes. Remove from the oven and spread with Chocolate Icing.

## Chocolate Icing

1/2 cup (1 stick) margarine
1 tablespoon baking cocoa
6 tablespoons milk
1 (1-pound) package confectioners' sugar
1 teaspoon vanilla extract
1 cup chopped pecans

Combine the margarine, baking cocoa and milk in a saucepan. Heat until smooth, stirring constantly. Stir in the confectioners' sugar, vanilla and pecans.

# Turtle Cake

1 (2-layer) package German chocolate cake mix
1 (14-ounce) package caramels
½ cup (1 stick) butter or margarine
1 (14-ounce) can sweetened condensed milk
1 cup (6 ounces) semisweet chocolate chips
1 cup pecans, chopped

*P*repare the cake batter using the package directions. Pour about half the batter into a greased and floured 9×13-inch cake pan. Bake at 350 degrees for 15 minutes. Remove from the oven and cool in the pan. Unwrap the caramels and place in a saucepan. Cook over medium heat until melted, stirring constantly. Add the butter. Heat until melted, stirring constantly. Remove from the heat. Add the condensed milk and mix well. Pour over the cooled cake. Sprinkle with the chocolate chips and pecans. Pour the remaining cake batter over the top. Bake for 30 minutes. Serve with ice cream.

SERVES 15

155

# Ice Cream Dessert

8 ounces graham crackers, crushed
1/2 cup (1 stick) butter, melted
1 cup confectioners' sugar
2 ounces unsweetened baking chocolate, melted
1/2 cup (1 stick) butter, melted
3 egg yolks
1 teaspoon vanilla extract
1/2 cup chopped walnuts or pecans
3 egg whites, stiffly beaten
1/2 gallon cherry vanilla ice cream, mint chocolate chip ice cream,
cookies and cream ice cream, or your favorite flavor

Mix the graham crackers and 1/2 cup butter in a bowl until coated.
Reserve 1/2 cup of the crumb mixture. Press the remaining crumb mixture
into a 9×12-inch baking dish. Bake at 350 degrees for 10 minutes.
Combine the confectioners' sugar, baking chocolate, 1/2 cup butter, egg
yolks, vanilla and walnuts in a bowl and mix well. Fold in the stiffly beaten
egg whites. Pour over the crust. Cover and freeze until firm. Let the ice
cream stand until softened. Spread the ice cream over the frozen layer.
Sprinkle with the reserved crumb mixture. Freeze until firm. Cut into
pieces to serve. Serve frozen.

SERVES 12

# Layered Oreo Ice Cream Dessert

1 (1-pound) can chocolate syrup
1 (14-ounce) can sweetened condensed milk
1/2 cup (1 stick) margarine
24 Oreo cookies
1/4 cup (1/2 stick) margarine, melted
1/2 gallon vanilla ice cream, softened
9 ounces whipped topping
Chopped nuts to taste

Combine the chocolate syrup, condensed milk and 1/2 cup margarine in a saucepan. Bring to a slight boil and reduce the heat. Simmer for 5 minutes, stirring constantly. Remove from the heat to cool. Crumble the cookies with a rolling pin and place in a bowl. Add 1/4 cup margarine and mix well. Pat into a long pan. Freeze for 30 minutes. Spread with the ice cream. Freeze for 30 minutes. Spread the cooled chocolate mixture over the ice cream. Freeze for 30 minutes. Spread the whipped topping over the top. Sprinkle with nuts. Freeze for 8 to 12 hours. Let stand at room temperature for a few minutes before serving.

SERVES 8 TO 10

157

# Black Bottom Pie

14 graham crackers, crushed
2 tablespoons butter, melted
1 tablespoon
  unflavored gelatin
1/4 cup cold water
5 egg yolks
1 egg white
3 tablespoons cornstarch
3/4 cup sugar
3 cups milk, scalded
1 1/2 ounces unsweetened
  chocolate, melted
1 teaspoon vanilla extract
4 egg whites
1/4 teaspoon cream of tartar
1/2 cup sugar
1 teaspoon vanilla extract

Mix the graham crackers and butter in a bowl. Press into a 9-inch pie plate. Bake at 350 degrees for 10 minutes or until brown. Remove from the oven to cool.

Soften the gelatin in the cold water. Beat the egg yolks and 1 egg white in a mixing bowl. Add the cornstarch and 3/4 cup sugar. Stir in the scalded milk. Pour into a double boiler. Cook until thickened, stirring constantly. Reserve 1 1/2 cups of the custard. Stir the softened gelatin into the remaining hot custard. Combine the reserved custard and melted chocolate in a bowl and mix well. Stir in 1 teaspoon vanilla. Let stand until cool. Pour into the piecrust. Chill in the refrigerator.

Beat 4 eggs whites at high speed in a mixing bowl until soft peaks form. Add the cream of tartar and 1/2 cup sugar gradually, beating constantly until stiff peaks form. Fold the stiffly beaten eggs whites and 1 teaspoon vanilla into the custard. Pour over the chilled chocolate layer. Chill until firm. Serve with whipped cream. (You may double the recipe and make in a square baking dish.)

SERVES 6

158

# Cream Cheese Brownie Pie

1 refrigerator pie pastry
8 ounces cream
   cheese, softened
3 tablespoons sugar
1 teaspoon vanilla extract
   1 egg

1 (15-ounce) package thick
   and fudgy hot fudge swirl
   deluxe brownie mix

1/4 cup vegetable oil
1 tablespoon water
2 eggs
1/2 cup chopped pecans
1 tablespoon water

*F*it the pastry into a 9-inch pie plate, trimming and fluting the edge. Prick the bottom with a fork. Bake at 350 degrees until golden brown. Combine the cream cheese, sugar, vanilla and 1 egg in a mixing bowl and beat until smooth. Reserve the hot fudge packet from the brownie mix for the topping. Combine the brownie mix, oil, 1 tablespoon water and 2 eggs in a large bowl. Beat for 50 strokes with a spoon. Spread 1/2 cup of the brownie mixture in the piecrust. Spoon the cream cheese mixture carefully over the brownie mixture. Spread the remaining brownie mixture evenly over the top. Sprinkle with the pecans. Bake at 350 degrees for 40 to 50 minutes or until the center is puffed and the crust is golden brown, covering the edge with strips of foil after 15 to 20 minutes to prevent over-browning. The pie may have cracks on the surface. Open the reserved hot fudge packet and squeeze into a small microwave-safe bowl. Microwave on High for 30 seconds. Stir in 1 tablespoon water. Drizzle over the pie. Chill for 3 hours or until completely cool. Store in the refrigerator.

SERVES 6 TO 8

159

# Mama's Chocolate Chess Pie

*Art for this recipe is shown on the cover.*

1½ cups sugar
2½ tablespoons baking cocoa
2 eggs
½ cup (1 stick) margarine, melted
1 teaspoon vanilla extract
1 (5-ounce) can evaporated milk
1 unbaked (10-inch) deep-dish pie shell

SERVES 6 TO 8

Mix the sugar, baking cocoa, eggs, margarine and vanilla in a bowl. Add the evaporated milk and mix well. Pour into the pie shell. Bake at 350 degrees for 30 to 40 minutes or until set. Cool completely before serving. Serve with whipped cream and chocolate syrup.

# Chocolate Chip Pie

1 cup sugar
½ cup flour
2 eggs, lightly beaten
½ cup (1 stick) margarine, melted
1 cup chopped pecans
1 cup (6 ounces) semisweet chocolate chips
1 teaspoon vanilla extract
1 unbaked (9-inch) pie shell

SERVES 6 TO 8

Combine the sugar, flour, eggs and margarine in a bowl and mix well. Stir in the pecans, chocolate chips and vanilla. Pour into the pie shell. Bake at 300 degrees for 45 minutes or until set. The pie will be soft until it cools, and then it will become firm.

# Chocolate Fudge Pie

¼ cup baking cocoa
¼ cup flour
1 cup sugar
½ cup (1 stick) margarine, melted
2 eggs, beaten
¼ cup milk
1 teaspoon vanilla extract
1 unbaked (9-inch) pie shell

Combine the baking cocoa, flour, sugar, margarine, eggs, milk and vanilla in a bowl and mix well. Pour into the pie shell. Bake at 325 degrees for 35 minutes or until set.

SERVES 6 TO 8

# Chocolate Pecan Pie

1 cup sugar
½ cup flour
2 eggs, beaten
½ cup (1 stick) margarine, melted and cooled
1 teaspoon vanilla extract
1 cup (6 ounces) chocolate chips
1 cup pecans
1 unbaked (9-inch) pie shell

Mix the sugar and flour in a bowl. Add the eggs and margarine and mix well. Stir in the vanilla. Stir in the chocolate chips and pecans. Pour into the pie shell. Bake at 350 degrees for 30 minutes or until set.

SERVES 6 TO 8

# Chocolate Strawberry Pie

1¼ cups graham cracker crumbs
3 tablespoons sugar
⅓ cup butter, melted
8 ounces cream cheese, softened
¼ cup packed brown sugar
½ teaspoon vanilla extract
3 ounces bittersweet chocolate, melted
1 cup whipping cream
1 cup sliced strawberries
1 cup (2 sticks) butter
1 ounce bittersweet chocolate

*Mix* the graham cracker crumbs, sugar and ⅓ cup butter in a bowl. Press into a 9-inch pie plate. Chill in the refrigerator. Beat the cream cheese, brown sugar and vanilla at medium speed in a mixing bowl until fluffy. Add the melted chocolate and beat well. Beat the whipping cream in a mixing bowl until soft peaks form. Fold into the chocolate mixture. Pour into the prepared pie plate. Chill for 8 to 12 hours. Arrange the strawberries over the top of the pie. Place 1 cup butter and 1 ounce chocolate in a sealable plastic bag. Microwave on High at 10-second intervals until melted. Snip a hole in the corner of the bag. Drizzle the chocolate mixture over the strawberries.

SERVES 6 TO 8

162

# Grandma's Chocolate Meringue Pie

1 cup sugar
3 tablespoons flour
2 tablespoons (heaping) baking cocoa
1 cup milk
3 egg yolks, lightly beaten
6 tablespoons margarine
1 tablespoon vanilla extract
1 baked (9-inch) pie shell
3 egg whites
6 tablespoons sugar
Pinch of cream of tartar
1 teaspoon vanilla extract

*M*ix 1 cup sugar, the flour and baking cocoa in a saucepan. Add the milk and egg yolks and mix well. Bring to a boil. Cook until thickened, stirring constantly. Add the margarine. Boil for 1 minute. Remove from the heat to cool. Stir in 1 tablespoon vanilla. Pour into the pie shell. Beat the egg whites at high speed in a mixing bowl until soft peaks form. Add 6 tablespoons sugar, the cream of tartar and 1 teaspoon vanilla gradually, beating for 3 to 5 minutes or until stiff peaks form. Spread over the filling, sealing to the edge. Bake at 300 degrees for 15 to 20 minutes or until golden brown. Remove from the oven to cool. Chill for 8 to 12 hours before serving.

SERVES 6 TO 8

# Papa's Fudge

4½ cups sugar
1 (12-ounce) can evaporated milk
1 cup (2 sticks) margarine
3 cups (18 ounces) chocolate chips
2 cups miniature marshmallows
1 teaspoon vanilla extract
2 cups chopped pecans

*B*ring the sugar, evaporated milk and margarine to a boil in a saucepan. Boil for 11 minutes, stirring constantly. Remove from the heat. Add the next 3 ingredients and beat until smooth. Stir in the pecans. Pour into a greased pan. Let stand at room temperature until set.

MAKES ABOUT 5 POUNDS

163

# Blondies with Pecans and Chocolate Chips

2 cups flour
1 teaspoon baking powder
3/4 teaspoon salt
1/4 teaspoon baking soda
10 tablespoons unsalted butter
2 cups packed light brown sugar
2 eggs
2 teaspoons vanilla extract
3/4 cup (4 1/2 ounces) semisweet chocolate chips
3/4 cup chopped pecans (about 3 ounces)

Mix the flour, baking powder, salt and baking soda in a medium bowl. Melt the butter in a large saucepan over low heat. Remove from the heat. Add the brown sugar and whisk to blend. Whisk in the eggs and vanilla. Stir in the flour mixture gradually. The batter will be thick. Spread the batter into a buttered and floured 9×13-inch baking pan. Sprinkle with the chocolate chips and pecans. Bake at 350 degrees for 25 minutes or until a tester inserted into the center comes out with moist crumbs attached. Cool in the pan on a wire rack. Cut into squares.

MAKES 2 DOZEN

## Brownies

1½ cups flour  1 cup vegetable oil
½ cup plus 2 teaspoons  4 eggs
  baking cocoa  2 teaspoons vanilla extract
2 cups sugar  1 cup chopped nuts
1 teaspoon salt

Sift the flour, baking cocoa, sugar and salt into a bowl. Add the oil and eggs and mix well. Stir in the vanilla and nuts. Spoon into a greased 9×13-inch baking pan. Bake at 350 degrees for 28 minutes or until the edges pull from the side of the pan. Serve warm with vanilla ice cream.

MAKES 2 DOZEN

## Reduced-Fat Brownies

6 tablespoons light margarine  1 cup flour
¼ cup baking cocoa  4 egg whites
½ cup sugar  1 teaspoon vanilla extract
1 cup packed brown sugar

Combine the margarine and baking cocoa in a microwave-safe cup. Microwave on High until melted. Combine the chocolate mixture, sugar, brown sugar, flour, egg whites and vanilla in a bowl and mix well. Pour into a baking pan coated with nonstick cooking spray. Bake at 350 degrees for 30 minutes.

MAKES 1½ DOZEN

# Chocolate Caramel Squares

1 (14-ounce) package caramels
⅓ cup evaporated milk
1 (2-layer) package German chocolate cake mix
¾ cup (1½ sticks) butter, melted
½ cup evaporated milk
1 cup chopped nuts
1 cup (6 ounces) chocolate chips

*U*nwrap the caramels and place in a microwave-safe bowl. Add ⅓ cup evaporated milk. Microwave on High until melted. Combine the cake mix, butter, ½ cup evaporated milk and nuts in a bowl and mix well. The batter will be thick. Spread ½ of the batter in a greased and floured 9×13-inch baking pan. Bake at 350 degrees for 15 minutes. Remove from the oven. Sprinkle with the chocolate chips. Spread the caramel mixture over the chocolate chips. Top with the remaining batter. Bake for 20 minutes. Cool slightly. Chill for 30 minutes. Cut into squares.

MAKES 4 DOZEN

166

# Buffalo Chips

4 cups flour
2 teaspoons baking soda
2 teaspoons baking powder
1 cup (2 sticks) margarine, softened
1 cup shortening
1 (1-pound) package light brown sugar
2 cups sugar
4 eggs
2 teaspoons vanilla extract
2 cups rolled oats
2 cups cornflakes
1 cup chopped pecans
1 cup coconut
2 cups (12 ounces) chocolate chips

Mix the flour, baking soda and baking powder together. Cream the margarine, shortening, brown sugar and sugar in a mixing bowl until light and fluffy. Add the eggs and vanilla and mix well. Stir in the flour mixture, oats, cornflakes, pecans, coconut and chocolate chips. Drop by heaping tablespoonfuls onto a nonstick cookie sheet and flatten with a spatula dipped in water. Bake at 350 degrees for 12 to 15 minutes or until golden brown. Cool on a wire rack. (You may substitute another flavor baking chip besides chocolate for the coconut.)

MAKES ABOUT 4 DOZEN

# Treasure Cookies

1½ cups graham cracker crumbs
½ cup flour
2 teaspoons baking powder
1 (14-ounce) can sweetened condensed milk
½ cup (1 stick) butter or margarine, softened
1⅓ cups flaked coconut
2 cups (12 ounces) semisweet chocolate chips
1 cup chopped walnuts

Mix the graham cracker crumbs, flour and baking powder in a small bowl. Combine the condensed milk and butter in a large mixing bowl and beat until smooth. Add the graham cracker crumb mixture and mix well. Stir in the coconut, chocolate chips and walnuts. Drop by rounded tablespoonfuls onto an ungreased cookie sheet. Bake at 375 degrees for 9 to 10 minutes or until light brown. Cool on a wire rack. Store, loosely covered, at room temperature.

MAKES 3 DOZEN

# Chocolate Chip Cookies

5 cups rolled oats
4 cups flour
1 teaspoon salt
2 teaspoons baking powder
2 teaspoons baking soda
2 cups (4 sticks) butter, softened
2 cups sugar
2 cups packed brown sugar
4 eggs
2 teaspoons vanilla extract
1 milk chocolate candy bar, grated
4 cups (24 ounces) chocolate chips
3 cups chopped pecans

*P*rocess the oats in a blender. Mix the processed oats, flour, salt, baking powder and baking soda in a bowl. Cream the butter, sugar and brown sugar in a large mixing bowl until light and fluffy. Add the eggs and vanilla and mix well. Add the oat mixture and mix well. Stir in the grated milk chocolate, chocolate chips and pecans. Drop by golf ball-size portions 2 inches apart onto an ungreased cookie sheet. Bake at 350 degrees for 6 minutes or until golden brown. Cool on a wire rack.

MAKES ABOUT 4 DOZEN

# Chocolate Peanut Butter Oatmeal Cookie Drops

2 cups sugar
3 tablespoons baking cocoa
½ cup milk
¼ cup (½ stick) margarine
½ cup peanut butter

1 teaspoon vanilla extract
3 cups quick-cooking oats
½ cup chopped pecans
(optional)

Mix the sugar, baking cocoa, milk and margarine in a saucepan. Boil for 1 minute, stirring constantly. Remove from the heat. Add the peanut butter, vanilla, oats and pecans and mix well. Drop by spoonfuls onto waxed paper. Let cool for 30 minutes.

MAKES 2 DOZEN

# Chocolate Sour Cream Frosting

2 cups (12 ounces) chocolate chips
1 (1-pound) package confectioners' sugar
1 cup sour cream
1 teaspoon vanilla extract

Melt the chocolate chips in a double boiler over hot water. Add ⅓ of the confectioners' sugar and beat until blended. Add the remaining confectioners' sugar and sour cream alternately, beating well after each addition. Stir in the vanilla.

MAKES ENOUGH FROSTING FOR A 2-LAYER CAKE

## Buttermilk Chocolate Icing

1/2 cup (1 stick) butter
1/4 cup baking cocoa
6 tablespoons buttermilk
1 (1-pound) package confectioners' sugar, sifted
1 teaspoon vanilla extract
1 cup chopped pecans

Combine the butter, baking cocoa and buttermilk in a heavy saucepan and mix well. Bring to a boil, stirring constantly. Remove from the heat. Add the confectioners' sugar, vanilla and pecans. Whip with a spoon for 2 minutes. Pour over your favorite sheet cake while still hot. The icing will thicken rapidly as it cools.

MAKES ABOUT 3 CUPS

## Chocolate Sauce

1/2 cup (1 stick) butter
2/3 cup chocolate chips
1 (12-ounce) can evaporated milk
2 cups confectioners' sugar
1 1/2 teaspoons vanilla extract

Melt the butter and chocolate chips in a heavy saucepan. Add the evaporated milk, confectioners' sugar and vanilla and mix well. Cook until thickened, stirring constantly.

MAKES 3 TO 4 CUPS

Blues legend Chester Arthur Burnett, "Howlin' Wolf" is a native son of Clay County. In 1995, The Howlin' Wolf Blues Society was established. That year, "The Howlin' Wolf" was inducted into the West Point Hall of Fame. Our hometown holds a memorial festival every year to honor his musical achievements. A memorial black granite statue of "The Howlin' Wolf" along with a memorial bench and marker honoring Lillie Handley Burnett, "Ms. Wolf," grace our park.

# DESSERTS

## CANCER CAMP

Every summer, a group of dedicated volunteers band together to create a magical week for children with cancer in Mississippi. At Camp Henry Pratt, just outside of Columbus, Mississippi, the unique camping experience is known as Camp Rising Sun. Our Junior Auxiliary chapter hosts the dance on Friday night every year, creating a magical night with decorations, food, a DJ, and photos of the children to keep as wonderful memories. They dance the night away, enjoying food, fun, and fellowship with fellow cancer victims. They leave the camp with a sense of hope, lots of love, and very special memories.

# Crème Brûlée

2 cups half-and-half
1 cup cream
2 tablespoons sugar
6 egg yolks
2 teaspoons vanilla extract
Brown sugar for topping

*H*eat the half-and-half, cream and sugar in a saucepan until the sugar dissolves, stirring constantly. Remove from the heat. Whip the egg yolks in a bowl. Whip a small amount of the hot cream mixture into the egg yolks. Add the egg yolk mixture to the cream mixture and mix well. Stir in the vanilla. Pour into 6 custard cups. Place the custard cups in a baking pan. Add enough water to the baking pan to come halfway up the side of the custard cups. Bake at 300 degrees for 50 to 60 minutes or until set. Remove from the baking pan and cool for 45 minutes. Sprinkle brown sugar over the top. Place back in the baking pan. Place ice around the custard cups. Broil 5 inches from the heat source until the brown sugar melts. Watch closely to prevent scorching. Remove from the oven and let stand until cool. Cover each custard cup with plastic wrap. Chill for 2 to 12 hours before serving.

SERVES 6

174

# Bread Pudding with Cognac Sauce

2 cups milk
1/4 cup (1/2 stick) butter
1/2 cup sugar
4 cups dry French bread cubes
1/2 cup raisins

2 eggs, beaten
1/8 teaspoon salt
1/2 teaspoon nutmeg
1 teaspoon vanilla extract
Cognac Sauce (below)

Scald the milk in a saucepan and remove from the heat. Add the butter and stir until melted. Stir in the sugar. Pour over the bread and raisins in a bowl. Let stand for 15 minutes. Add the eggs, salt, nutmeg and vanilla and mix well. Spoon into a 1 1/2-quart baking dish. Bake at 350 degrees for 35 minutes. Serve with Cognac Sauce.

SERVES 4 TO 6

## Cognac Sauce

1/2 cup (1 stick) butter, softened
2 cups confectioners' sugar
1/4 cup cognac

Cream the butter and confectioners' sugar in a mixing bowl until fluffy. Add the cognac gradually, beating constantly until smooth.

# Rice Pudding

4 eggs
1 cup sugar
Dash of salt
2 1/3 cups milk, scalded
1 teaspoon vanilla extract
1 tablespoon cinnamon
2 tablespoons butter, melted
2 cups cooked white rice
Dash of nutmeg

Beat the eggs in a mixing bowl until pale yellow. Beat in the sugar and salt. Add the milk gradually, beating constantly. Add the vanilla, cinnamon and butter and beat well. Stir in the cooked rice. Pour into a 9x11-inch deep baking dish. Sprinkle with nutmeg. Bake at 350 degrees for 30 minutes.

SERVES 6 TO 8

# Cherry Delight

1 (21-ounce) can cherry pie filling
1 (20-ounce) can crushed pineapple, drained
1 (2-layer) package yellow cake mix
1/2 cup (1 stick) butter, melted
1 cup chopped pecans

Layer the pie filling, pineapple, dry cake mix, butter and pecans in the order listed in a 9x13-inch baking dish. Bake at 325 degrees for 1 hour. Serve with ice cream.

SERVES 8

# Strawberry Pizza

2 cups flour
1 cup (2 sticks) margarine, melted
1 cup chopped pecans
8 ounces cream cheese, softened
3 cups confectioners' sugar
12 ounces whipped topping
1 cup sugar
3 tablespoons cornstarch
1 cup water
1 (3-ounce) package strawberry gelatin
2 pints fresh strawberries

*M*ix the flour, margarine and pecans in a bowl. Press into a 9×12-inch baking dish. Bake at 350 degrees for 20 minutes or until light brown. Remove from the oven to cool. Beat the cream cheese and confectioners' sugar in a mixing bowl until smooth. Fold in the whipped topping. Spread over the baked layer, bringing up the sides to form a shell. Bring the sugar, cornstarch and water to a boil in a saucepan. Boil for 1 minute. Stir in the gelatin until dissolved. Remove from the heat to cool. Stir in the strawberries. Spoon on top of the cheese mixture. Chill, covered, until set. Store in the refrigerator.

SERVES 12

# Berry Rich Ice Cream

1 quart fresh strawberries
1 (12-ounce) can
  strawberry soda
2 (14-ounce) cans sweetened
  condensed milk

1 cup heavy cream
1½ cups sugar
1 tablespoon vanilla extract
2 cups half-and-half
Milk

SERVES 8 TO 10

Rinse the strawberries and pat dry. Remove the hulls from the strawberries. Chill all of the ingredients in the freezer for 30 minutes. Chop the strawberries in a blender or food processor. Combine the soda, condensed milk, cream, sugar, vanilla and half-and-half in a bowl and mix well. Stir in the strawberries. Pour into an ice cream freezer container. Add enough milk to reach the fill line. Freeze using the manufacturer's directions. (You may substitute another fruit and soda, such as peach.)

# Peach Ice Cream

8 peaches
¾ cup sugar
5 cups milk
2 cups heavy cream

2 cups half-and-half
1 tablespoon vanilla extract
6 eggs
2 cups sugar

Mash the peaches in a bowl. Add ¾ cup sugar and mix well. Blend the milk, cream, half-and-half and vanilla in a bowl. Beat the eggs in a mixing bowl until light. Add 2 cups sugar gradually, beating constantly. Add the milk mixture and mix well. Stir in the peach mixture. Pour into a 1-gallon ice cream freezer container. Freeze using the manufacturer's directions.

MAKES 1 GALLON

# Cheesecake

1²/₃ cups graham cracker crumbs

¹/₃ cup margarine, melted

40 ounces cream cheese

1¹/₂ cups sugar

3 eggs

2¹/₂ teaspoons vanilla extract

8 ounces cream cheese, softened

¹/₂ (1-pound) package confectioners' sugar

1¹/₂ teaspoons vanilla extract

12 ounces whipped topping

Mix the graham cracker crumbs and margarine in bowl. Press firmly on the bottom and 1 inch up the side of a springform pan. Bake at 350 degrees for 5 minutes. Remove from the oven to cool.

Let 40 ounces cream cheese stand at room temperature for 2 hours to soften. Beat the cream cheese at high speed in a mixing bowl until light and fluffy. Add the sugar ¹/₂ cup at a time, beating well after each addition. Add the eggs 1 at a time, beating well after each addition. Stir in 2¹/₂ teaspoons vanilla. Pour into the cooled crust.

Bake at 350 degrees for 30 minutes. Turn off the oven and partially open the oven door. Let stand in the oven for 45 minutes. Remove from the oven. Cover with paper towels and let cool in a draft-free place. Chill, covered, for at least 8 hours.

Beat 8 ounces cream cheese in a mixing bowl until fluffy. Add the confectioners' sugar and 1¹/₂ teaspoons vanilla and beat until smooth. Fold in the whipped topping. Chill, covered, until ready to serve.

To serve, remove the sides of the springform pan and place the cheesecake on a cake plate. Spread the cream cheese mixture over the cheesecake. (Note: You may also add cherries or a fruit topping of choice. Instead of the graham cracker crust, try using 1²/₃ cups pecan sandies instead; you do not have to add butter or bake.)

SERVES 15

179

# Apple Cake

4 cups chopped peeled Delicious apples
1 cup broken pecans
2 cups sugar
3 cups flour
2 teaspoons baking soda
1/2 teaspoon vanilla extract
1/2 teaspoon cinnamon
1/2 teaspoon nutmeg
1 cup vegetable oil
2 eggs, beaten

SERVES 16

*T*oss the apples with the pecans and sugar in a bowl. Let stand for 1 hour, stirring frequently. Mix the flour, baking soda, vanilla, cinnamon and nutmeg in a bowl. Add the oil and eggs and mix well. Add to the apple mixture and mix well. Spoon into a greased and floured tube pan. Bake at 350 degrees for 1 1/4 hours. Cool and invert onto a serving plate.

# Blueberry Pound Cake

1 (16-ounce) can blueberries
1 (2-layer) package butter cake mix
8 ounces cream cheese, softened
1 (4-ounce) package vanilla instant pudding mix
3 eggs
1/2 cup vegetable oil
1/4 cup (1/2 stick) butter, softened
2 cups confectioners' sugar

Drain the blueberries, reserving the juice. Combine the cake mix, cream cheese, pudding mix, eggs, oil and butter in a mixing bowl and beat until smooth. Fold in the blueberries. Spoon into a greased and floured tube pan. Bake at 325 degrees for 1 hour.

Mix the confectioners' sugar with enough of the reserved blueberry juice to form a glaze. Pour over the hot cake. Cool and invert onto a serving plate.

SERVES 16

181

# Elvis Presley Cake

1 (2-layer) package butter cake mix
½ cup sugar
1 (20-ounce) can crushed pineapple
8 ounces cream cheese, softened
¼ cup (½ stick) butter, softened
1 (1-pound) package confectioners' sugar
1 teaspoon vanilla extract
½ cup chopped pecans (optional)

*P*repare and bake the cake using the package directions for a 9x13-inch cake pan. Bring the sugar and undrained pineapple to a boil in a saucepan, stirring constantly. Prick holes in the hot cake. Pour the pineapple mixture over the top. Let stand until completely cool.

Beat the cream cheese and butter in a mixing bowl until smooth and creamy. Add the confectioners' sugar and vanilla and beat well. Stir in the pecans. Spread over the cake. Store, covered, in the refrigerator. (Note: This cake is best prepared the day before serving to allow the pineapple mixture time to soak into the cake, making it very moist.)

SERVES 15

## Lemon Cake

1 (2-layer) package lemon cake mix
12 ounces whipped topping
1 (14-ounce) can sweetened condensed milk
1 (6-ounce) can frozen lemonade concentrate
Few drops of yellow food coloring

*P*repare and bake the cake using the package directions for 3 or 4 round cake pans. Cool on wire racks. Combine the whipped topping, condensed milk, lemonade concentrate and food coloring in a bowl and mix until smooth. Spread between the layers and over the top and side of the cake. Garnish with sliced lemon or mint.

SERVES 15

## Piña Colada Cake

1 (2-layer) package yellow cake mix
1 cup shredded coconut
1 (8-ounce) can cream of coconut
1 (20-ounce) can crushed pineapple, drained
12 ounces whipped topping

*P*repare and bake the cake mix using the package directions for a 9×13-inch cake pan and adding the coconut. Remove the cake from the oven. Pierce holes in the hot cake with a fork. Pour the cream of coconut and pineapple over the hot cake. Let stand until cool. Spread the whipped topping over the top. Garnish with shredded coconut and pecans. Store in the refrigerator.

SERVES 15

# Pineapple Carrot Cake

2 cups flour
2 teaspoons baking powder
1½ teaspoons baking soda
1 teaspoon salt
2 teaspoons cinnamon
1½ cups vegetable oil
2 cups sugar
4 eggs

1 teaspoon vanilla extract
2 cups grated carrots
1 (6-ounce) can crushed
pineapple, drained
¾ cup chopped pecans
Cream Cheese Frosting
(below)
Chopped pecans for sprinkling

Sift the flour, baking powder, baking soda, salt and cinnamon together. Beat the oil, sugar and eggs in a mixing bowl. Add the flour mixture and mix well. Stir in the vanilla, carrots, pineapple and ¾ cup pecans. Spoon into 3 greased and floured 9-inch cake pans. Bake at 325 degrees for 30 to 35 minutes or until the layers test done. Cool in the pans for 10 minutes. Remove to wire racks to cool completely. Spread Cream Cheese Frosting between the layers and over the top and side of the cake. Sprinkle the top with chopped pecans.

**SERVES 12**

## Cream Cheese Frosting

8 ounces cream cheese, softened
½ cup (1 stick) margarine, softened
1 (1-pound) package confectioners' sugar
2 teaspoons vanilla extract

Beat the cream cheese and margarine in a mixing bowl until light. Add the confectioners' sugar and vanilla and beat until smooth.

# Seven-Up Cake

1 (2-layer) package lemon supreme cake mix
1 (4-ounce) package lemon instant pudding mix
4 eggs
1 cup vegetable oil
10 ounces 7-Up
Pineapple Coconut Frosting (below)

Combine the cake mix, pudding mix, eggs, oil and soda in a mixing bowl and mix well. Spoon into 2 greased and floured 9-inch cake pans. Bake at 350 degrees for 30 minutes or until the layers test done. Cool in the pans for 10 minutes. Remove to wire racks to cool completely. Spread Pineapple Coconut Frosting between the layers and over the top and side of the cake.

SERVES 12

# Pineapple Coconut Frosting

1/2 cup (1 stick) butter
1 (20-ounce) can crushed pineapple, drained
3 egg yolks
2 cups sugar
3 tablespoons flour
1 (7-ounce) can flaked coconut

Melt the butter in a saucepan over low heat. Stir in the pineapple, egg yolks, sugar, flour and coconut and mix well. Cook until thickened, stirring constantly.

# Apple Pie

4 to 6 Granny Smith apples, peeled and sliced
1 unbaked (9-inch) pie shell
2 tablespoons butter
  1/2 cup sugar
  1/2 teaspoon cinnamon
2 cups shredded coconut
  1/2 cup evaporated milk
  1/2 teaspoon salt
1 egg, lightly beaten
  1/2 cup sugar

*Layer* the apples in the pie shell. Dot with the butter. Sprinkle with a mixture of 1/2 cup sugar and the cinnamon. Bake at 350 degrees for 15 to 20 minutes or until the apples are tender. Remove from the oven. Sprinkle with the coconut. Mix the evaporated milk, salt, egg and 1/2 cup sugar in a bowl. Pour over the pie. Return to the oven. Bake for 7 to 12 minutes or until brown. Watch carefully to prevent over-browning. Serve with whipped cream, ice cream or shredded cheese.

SERVES 6 TO 8

186

# Caramel Pecan Cheesecake Pie

20 caramels
2 tablespoons milk
1/2 cup chopped pecans
1 (9-inch) graham cracker
   pie shell

16 ounces cream cheese,
   softened
1/2 cup sugar
1 1/2 teaspoons vanilla extract
2 eggs

*U*nwrap the caramels. Combine with the milk in a saucepan. Heat until the caramels melt, stirring constantly. Stir in the pecans. Pour into the pie shell. Beat the cream cheese, sugar and vanilla in a mixing bowl until smooth. Add the eggs and beat well. Spread over the caramel layer. Bake at 350 degrees for 40 minutes.

SERVES 6 TO 8

# Buttermilk Coconut Pie

1 1/2 cups sugar
1/2 cup flour
1/2 cup (1 stick) margarine,
   melted
3 eggs, beaten

1/2 cup buttermilk
1 teaspoon vanilla extract
1 1/2 cups shredded coconut
1 unbaked (9-inch) pie shell

*C*ombine the sugar, flour, margarine, eggs, buttermilk and vanilla in a mixing bowl and mix well. Stir in the coconut. Pour into the pie shell. Bake at 325 degrees for 1 hour.

SERVES 6 TO 8

# Coconut Cream Pie

1 cup sugar
1/4 cup flour
2 cups milk
3 egg yolks
2 tablespoons butter
1 teaspoon vanilla extract
1 (6-ounce) package
    shredded coconut
1 baked (10-inch) deep-dish
    pie shell
1 tablespoon cornstarch
1/4 cup sugar
1/2 cup boiling water
3 egg whites
Pinch of salt
1 teaspoon vanilla extract

Mix 1 cup sugar and the flour in a heavy saucepan. Stir in the milk and egg yolks. Cook over medium heat until thickened, stirring constantly. Add the butter, 1 teaspoon vanilla and coconut and mix well. Pour into the baked pie shell.

Dissolve the cornstarch and 1/4 cup sugar in the boiling water in a saucepan. Cook until thick and clear, stirring constantly. Remove from the heat. Let stand until cool. Beat the egg whites at high speed in a mixing bowl until soft peaks form. Add the sugar mixture, salt and 1 teaspoon vanilla gradually, beating constantly until stiff peaks form. Spread over the pie, sealing to the edge. Bake at 350 degrees for 10 to 15 minutes or until golden brown.

SERVES 6 TO 8

# Lemon Pie

1/2 cup (1 stick) margarine
1 cup self-rising flour
1/2 cup pecans
8 ounces cream cheese, softened
1 cup confectioners' sugar
12 ounces whipped topping
2 (14-ounce) cans sweetened condensed milk
6 egg yolks
3/4 cup lemon juice
Grated lemon zest

Melt the margarine in a saucepan. Add the flour and pecans and mix well. Press into a pie plate. Bake at 325 degrees for 20 minutes. Beat the cream cheese, confectioners' sugar and 1/2 of the whipped topping in a mixing bowl until smooth. Add the condensed milk, egg yolks, lemon juice and lemon zest and mix well. Pour into the prepared pie plate. Spread the remaining whipped topping over the pie, sealing to the edge. Store in the refrigerator. (Note: If you are concerned about using raw egg yolks, use yolks from eggs pasteurized in their shells, which are sold at some specialty food stores, or use an equivalent amount of pasteurized egg substitute.)

SERVES 6 TO 8

189

# Pecan Pie

⅓ cup margarine
3 eggs
1 cup sugar
⅔ cup dark corn syrup
1 cup pecans
1 unbaked (9-inch) pie shell

SERVES 6 TO 8

*Melt* the margarine in a saucepan. Beat the eggs with a fork in a bowl. Add the margarine, sugar, corn syrup and pecans and mix well. Pour into the pie shell. Bake at 400 degrees for 10 minutes. Reduce the oven temperature to 325 degrees. Bake for 45 minutes or until the center of the pie is set.

# Strawberry Pie

1 cup sugar
1 cup water
2 tablespoons cornstarch
3 tablespoons strawberry gelatin
Sliced fresh strawberries
1 baked (9-inch) pie shell

SERVES 6 TO 8

*Combine* the sugar, water and cornstarch in a saucepan and mix well. Cook until thickened and clear, stirring constantly. Remove from the heat. Add the gelatin and stir until dissolved. Stir in the strawberries. Spoon into the baked pie shell. Chill until firm.

# Pumpkin Brownies

2 cups flour
1 tablespoon pumpkin pie spice
2 teaspoons cinnamon
2 teaspoons baking powder
1 teaspoon baking soda
1/2 teaspoon salt

1 (16-ounce) can pumpkin
4 eggs
2 cups sugar
3/4 cup vegetable oil
2 teaspoons vanilla extract
Cream Cheese Frosting (below)

*M*ix the flour, pumpkin pie spice, cinnamon, baking powder, baking soda and salt together. Combine the pumpkin, eggs, sugar, oil and vanilla in a bowl and mix well. Stir the flour mixture into the pumpkin mixture. Pour into a 10×15-inch baking pan. Bake at 350 degrees for 20 to 25 minutes or until the edges pull from the side of the pan. Remove from the oven to cool. Frost with Cream Cheese Frosting.

MAKES 5 TO 6 DOZEN

# Cream Cheese Frosting

6 tablespoons butter, softened
3 ounces cream cheese, softened
1 teaspoon vanilla extract
1 teaspoon milk
1/8 teaspoon salt
1 1/2 to 2 cups confectioners' sugar

*B*eat the butter and cream cheese in a mixing bowl until creamy. Add the vanilla, milk, salt and confectioners' sugar and beat until smooth.

# Chess Squares

1 (2-layer) package yellow   1 (1-pound) package
   cake mix                     confectioners' sugar
½ cup (1 stick) butter,    8 ounces cream cheese,
   softened                   softened
   1 egg   3 eggs

Mix the cake mix, butter and 1 egg in a bowl. Press into a 9×13-inch baking pan. Cream the confectioners' sugar and cream cheese in a mixing bowl. Add 3 eggs and beat until fluffy. Spread in the prepared pan. Bake at 325 degrees for 50 minutes. Remove from the oven to cool. Cut into squares. (Note: For Lemon Chess Squares, use lemon cake mix.)

MAKES 2 TO 3 DOZEN

# Tea Cakes

2 cups self-rising flour   ⅓ cup milk
⅔ cup sugar            1 teaspoon vanilla extract
½ cup shortening     1 egg

Mix the flour and sugar in a bowl. Beat the shortening, milk, vanilla and egg in a bowl until smooth. Add the flour mixture and mix well. Shape into a ball, adding additional flour if needed. Roll into a circle the desired thickness on a lightly floured surface. Cut with cookie cutters into desired shapes. Place on a cookie sheet. Bake at 350 degrees for 10 to 15 minutes or until light brown. Cool on a wire rack. Frost if desired.

MAKES 2 DOZEN

# Heath Bar Cookies

1¾ cups flour
1 teaspoon salt
¾ teaspoon baking soda
¾ cup (¾ stick) butter-flavor shortening
1¼ cups packed light brown sugar
2 tablespoons milk
1 tablespoon vanilla extract
1 egg
1 cup crushed Heath candy bars

Mix the flour, salt and baking soda together. Combine the shortening, brown sugar, milk and vanilla in a large mixing bowl and beat at medium speed until blended. Beat in the egg. Add the flour mixture and mix just until blended. Stir in the crushed candy bars. Drop by rounded tablespoonfuls 3 inches apart onto an ungreased cookie sheet. Bake 1 baking sheet at a time at 375 degrees for 8 to 10 minutes for chewy cookies or 11 to 13 minutes for crisp cookies. Cool on the cookie sheet for 2 minutes. Remove to pieces of foil to cool completely.

MAKES 2 DOZEN

# Oatmeal White Chippers

1 cup flour
1 teaspoon baking soda
3/4 cup (1 1/2 sticks) margarine, softened
1/2 cup sugar
1/2 cup packed brown sugar
1 egg
2 1/2 cups rolled oats
1 1/2 cups coarsely chopped vanilla bark
1/2 cup finely chopped almonds

Mix the flour and baking soda together. Beat the margarine in a mixing bowl until creamy. Add the sugar and brown sugar and beat until fluffy. Beat in the egg. Add the flour mixture and beat well. Stir in the oats, vanilla bark and almonds. Drop by rounded tablespoonfuls 3 inches apart onto an ungreased cookie sheet and flatten slightly. Bake at 375 degrees for 10 minutes. Cool on a wire rack.

MAKES 3 DOZEN

# Peanut Butter Cookies

3 cups flour
1 teaspoon baking soda
1 teaspoon salt
1 cup packed brown sugar
1 cup sugar
1 cup shortening
2 eggs
1 cup peanut butter
1 teaspoon vanilla extract

Mix the flour, baking soda and salt together. Beat the brown sugar, sugar and shortening in a mixing bowl until fluffy. Add the eggs, peanut butter and vanilla and mix well. Beat in the flour mixture. Roll into small balls. Place on a cookie sheet. Press each with a fork to form a crisscross pattern. Bake at 375 degrees for 10 to 15 minutes or until golden brown. Cool on a wire rack.

MAKES 2½ DOZEN

# Orange Balls

1 (12-ounce) package vanilla wafers
½ cup (1 stick) margarine, softened
1 (6-ounce) can frozen orange juice concentrate
1 (1-pound) package confectioners' sugar
1 cup chopped nuts
1 (14-ounce) package shredded coconut

Crush the vanilla wafers and place in a bowl. Add the margarine, orange juice concentrate and confectioners' sugar. Fold in the nuts. Shape into small balls. Roll in the coconut. Store, covered, in an airtight container in the refrigerator.

MAKES 4 TO 5 DOZEN

# Grandmother's Peanut Brittle

2 cups sugar
1/4 cup water
3/4 cup corn syrup
Pinch of salt
2 cups raw peanuts
4 teaspoons baking soda

Combine the sugar, water, corn syrup and salt in a double boiler and mix well. Cook until the sugar melts. Add the raw peanuts. Do not stir. Cook to 300 to 310 degrees on a candy thermometer, hard-crack stage. The mixture will be golden brown around the edge of the pan. Remove from the heat. Stir in the baking soda quickly. Pour onto a buttered tray. The mixture will harden quickly and will not stick if cooked enough. Let stand until cool. Break into pieces.

MAKES ABOUT 2 POUNDS

# COOKBOOK COMMITTEE

Project Chair: Cindy Davis
Co-Chair: Lee Ann Glusenkamp

# CONTRIBUTORS

*Special thanks to all active, associate, and life members who contributed to the publication of this cookbook.*

## ACTIVE MEMBERS

Mrs. William Allen *(Kimberly Ray)*
Mrs. Shane Alpe *(Kristie Kemp)*
Mrs. Jamey Ballard *(Katie Sims)*
Mrs. Sherman Berry *(Amy Gray)*
Mrs. Wilkes Bryan *(Amy Word)*
Mrs. Kenneth Burns *(Autumn Linton)*
Mrs. Chris Chambless *(Elisha Pace)*
Mrs. Bobby Cole *(Melissa Sanders)*
Mrs. Chris Davis *(Sharon Dean)*
Mrs. John Freeman *(Sherry Stewart)*
Miss Kerrie Gentry *(Kerrie Gentry)*
Mrs. Scott Hallmark *(Susan Donahoo)*

Mrs. Thomas Bradley Judson *(Molly Litchfield)*
Mrs. Justin Knowles *(Julie Sloan)*
Mrs. James Ashley Kuhn *(Jennifer Richmond)*
Mrs. Sam Marshall *(Danielle Holt)*
Mrs. Garnett McDaniels *(Garnett Tubb)*
Mrs. Mark Norman *(Paula Stacy)*
Mrs. Shasta Plunkett *(Rebecca Duke)*
Mrs. Brian Roberts *(Nikole Kaiser)*
Mrs. Jason Rustin *(Rebecca Bailey)*
Mrs. G. Scott Trull *(Carol Gary)*
Mrs. Ken Wilbourne *(Dawn Sanders)*
Mrs. Wes Williamson *(Michelle Simmons)*

198

# CONTRIBUTORS

## ASSOCIATE MEMBERS

Mrs. Jason Armstrong (*Tami Williams*)

Mrs. Bill Baer (*Sharon Dahlen*)

Mrs. Mark Bernegger (*Zandy Hurst*)

Mrs. Jerry Blackwell (*Anita Christian*)

Mrs. Heath Brand (*Sheila Gwathney*)

Mrs. George Brown (*Missy McVay*)

Mrs. Barry Bryan (*Paula Bird*)

Mrs. Bill Burris (*Vickie Mashburne*)

Mrs. Billy Caskey (*Joy Moore*)

Mrs. John Caskey (*Martha Lott*)

Mrs. Paul Caskey (*Kimberly Simmons*)

Mrs. Gene Childress (*Wendy East*)

Mrs. Bill Colloredo (*Maureen Lenahan*)

Mrs. Danny Comer (*Kathy Lyon*)

Mrs. Darrell Daigre (*Lisa Elkins*)

Mrs. Andy Davis (*Cindy O'Barr*)

Mrs. Philip Dimino (*Mary Kline*)

Mrs. Kevin Donahoo (*Donna Andrews*)

Mrs. Michael East (*Tiffany Childress*)

Mrs. Gary Echols (*Dee Sanders*)

Mrs. Todd Glusenkamp (*Lee Ann Page*)

Mrs. Andy Gray (*Julie Campbell*)

Mrs. Ben Perry Green (*Sara Claire Hathorn*)

Mrs. Lath Hairston (*Kaycee Cooper*)

Mrs. Joey Hays (*Stacy Bruce*)

Mrs. Kenneth Hinshaw (*Deborah Fowler*)

Mrs. Peter T. Hodo III (*Cynthia Marshall*)

Ms.   Andrea Holcombe (*Andrea Nester*)

Mrs. Philip Gary Hudson (*Connie Nash*)

Mrs. Luke Lummus (*Susan McTaggart*)

Mrs. Rick May (*Cindy Williams*)

Mrs. Phil McClellan (*Ann Bryan*)

Mrs. Lee McCormick (*Robin Young*)

Mrs. Kenneth Millsaps (*Connie Davis*)

Mrs. Steve Mitchener (*Becky Pongetti*)

Mrs. Les Pollard (*Gale Pate*)

Mrs. Ronald E. Powell (*Diann Barrett*)

Mrs. George Purnell (*Luann Green*)

Mrs. Paul Purnell (*Jacque Landes*)

Mrs. Mark Randle (*Lisa Watson*)

Mrs. Larry Rice (*Judy Fulgham*)

Mrs. Scott Ross (*Donna Hill*)

Mrs. Art Shirley (*Becky Rodgers*)

Mrs. David Shope (*Lynne Hood*)

Mrs. Ben Smith (*Jane Davis*)

Mrs. Harry Stevens (*Gayle Jasper*)

Mrs. Mort Stroud (*Beth Christian*)

Mrs. Jim Trenor (*Bobbie Tedder*)

# CONTRIBUTORS

## LIFE MEMBERS

Mrs. Marie Barron (*Marie Alford*)
Mrs. Monte Brasfield (*Suzanne Boozer*)
Mrs. Edna Earl Carothers (*Edna Earl Locke*)
Mrs. James Carothers (*Mary Davis*)
Mrs. Kyle Chandler III (*Susan Whetstone*)
Mrs. Charles Cliett (*Grace Campbell*)
Mrs. Hugh Cooper (*Carolyn Justice*)
Mrs. H. P. Daggett (*Helen Lanham*)
Mrs. Charles Dimino (*Becky Raley*)
Mrs. D. C. Dimino (*Vicki Perkins*)
Mrs. Larry Dunham (*Jo Ann Reid*)
Mrs. W. H. Edwards, Jr. (*Jackie Reese*)
Mrs. Chet Gregg (*Kay Trulove*)
Mrs. Toxey D. Haas (*Diane Lusk*)
Mrs. Gary Hamilton (*Judy Stembridge*)
Mrs. James Harper (*Ann White*)
Mrs. Edgar Harris (*Donna Smith*)
Ms. Anna Hart Hazard
   (*Anna Hart McFarland*)
Mrs. Gordon Hazard (*Sara Stevens*)
Mrs. Mike Henson (*Billie Dee Kirkpatrick*)
Mrs. Frank Hopper (*Diane Aust*)
Mrs. John C. Jameson III (*Janet Turnage*)
Mrs. J. C. Johnson (*Hortense Moore*)
Mrs. Lee Lox (*Lee Allen*)
Mrs. Edward Lyon (*Brucie Doughty*)
Mrs. Thomas McMullan (*Dorothy Smith*)

Mrs. Roger Merchant (*Jane Tucker*)
Mrs. Billy Milican (*Loretta Sanders*)
Mrs. Randolph Millard (*Grace Evens Justice*)
Mrs. Ray Millard (*Nina Lockett*)
Mrs. Raymond Millard, Jr. (*Bird C. Calvert*)
Miss Malinda Montgomery
   (*Malinda Montgomery*)
Mrs. Paul Morches (*Martha Gunn*)
Mrs. Bobby Murphy (*Mary Blankenship*)
Mrs. Danny Rainey (*Susan Fewel*)
Ms. Lynne Posey (*Lynne Young*)
Mrs. Joe Portera (*Susan Richardson*)
Mrs. Hampton Phyfer (*Jo Sneed*)
Mrs. Tony J. Rosetti, Jr. (*Lona Lewellen*)
Mrs. Wilson Simmons (*Clara Lou Thompson*)
Mrs. W. J. Staggers, Jr. (*Christabel Buck*)
Ms. Elaine Tiffin (*Elaine Tiffin*)
Mrs. Steve Tribble (*Thea Kay Doss*)
Mrs. Bud Tumlinson (*Bobbie Martin*)
Mrs. P. I. Turner (*Mildred Vandergrift*)
Mrs. Marvin Turnipseed (*Jane Brock*)
Mrs. Albert Walker (*Eloise Frego*)
Mrs. Rufus Ward (*Karen Threadgill*)
Mrs. Fred B. Weems (*Stacy Randall*)
Mrs. Ralph Weems III (*Sherrill Shannon*)
Mrs. Garland Wray (*Beulah Blankenship*)
Mrs. Caradine Young (*Charlotte Wimberley*)

# INDEX

# INDEX

# INDEX

# INDEX

# INDEX

# DOWN HOME

Treasured Recipes *from* Our House to Yours

West Point Junior Auxiliary

P.O. Box 45

West Point, Mississippi 39773

| YOUR ORDER | QUANTITY | TOTAL |
|---|---|---|
| *Down Home* at $24.95 per book | $ | $ |
| Mississippi residents add 7% sales tax | $ | $ |
| Postage and handling at $4.00 per book | TOTAL | $ |

Please make check payable to the West Point Junior Auxiliary.

Name

Street Address

City                                State                    Zip

Telephone

*Photocopies will be accepted.*